Twelfth Edition

THE NEW YORK NOTARY LAW PRIMER

*All the hard-to-find information
every New York Notary Public
needs to know!*

National Notary Association

Published by

National Notary Association
9350 De Soto Avenue
Chatsworth, CA 91311-4926
(800) 876-6827
Fax: (818) 700-0920
Website: www.NationalNotary.org
Email: nna@NationalNotary.org

The information in this *Primer* is correct and current at the time
of its publication, although new laws, regulations and rulings may
subsequently affect the validity of certain sections. This information
is provided to aid comprehension of state Notary Public requirements
and should not be construed as legal advice. Please consult an
attorney for inquiries relating to legal matters.

Twelfth Edition ©2014
First Edition ©1987

ISBN: 978-1-59767-142-2

Table
of Contents

For the latest updates on state laws
and requirements, please visit

www.NationalNotary.org/Primer-Updates

Have a Tough Notary Question?

If you were a National Notary Association member, you could
get the answer to that difficult question. Join the NNA® and your
membership includes access to the NNA Hotline* and live Notary
experts providing the latest Notary information regarding laws,
rules and regulations.

Hours
Monday–Friday   5:00 a.m.–7:00 p.m. (PT)
Saturdays   5:00 a.m.–5:00 p.m. (PT)

NNA Hotline Toll-Free Phone Number: 1-888-876-0827

After hours you can leave a message or email our experts at
Hotline@NationalNotary.org and they will respond the next business day.

*Access to the NNA Hotline is for National Notary Association members and
NNA Hotline subscribers only. Call and become a member today.

Introduction

You are to be commended on your interest in New York Notary law! Purchasing The *New York Notary Law Primer* identifies you as a conscientious professional who takes your official responsibilities seriously.

In few fields is the expression "more to it than meets the eye" more true than in Notary law. What often appears on the surface to be a simple procedure may, in fact, have important legal considerations. *The New York Notary Law Primer* is a resource created to help you decipher the state laws that affect notarization as well as to acquaint you with prudent Notary practices in general.

This edition of *The New York Notary Law Primer* includes administrative rules providing guidelines for electronic notarization, listing terms Notaries may not use when advertising in a foreign language, and offering disclaimers which must be posted in non-English advertisements for Notary services in simplified Chinese, traditional Chinese, Spanish, Korean and Haitian Creole.

While *The New York Notary Law Primer* begins with informative chapters on how to become a Notary Public, what tools a Notary needs, often-asked questions and critical steps in notarization, the heart of the book is the chapter titled "Notary Laws Explained." Here, we take you through New York's Notary laws and put them in easy-to-understand terms. Every pertinent section of the statutes is analyzed and explained, as are topics not covered by New York law but nonetheless of vital concern to you as a Notary.

For handy reference, at the end of the *Primer* we have reprinted the *Notary Public License Law* (NPLL), the New York Department of State's compilation of laws relating to Notaries

Public. In addition, we have included addresses and phone numbers of Department of State offices, New York county clerks' offices and Bureaus of Vital Statistics for all U.S. states and jurisdictions. Finally, we have compiled a list of nations that are parties to the Hague Convention, a treaty which simplifies the process of authenticating notarized documents.

Whether you're about to be commissioned for the first time or are a longtime Notary, we're sure that *The New York Notary Law Primer* will provide you with new insight into and understanding of your official duties. Your improved comprehension of New York's Notary laws will naturally result in your greater competence as a professional Notary Public.

> Milton G. Valera
> Chairman
> National Notary Association

How to Become a New York Notary Public

1. Ensure that you comply with the basic qualifications for a New York Notary commission.

You must meet the basic requirements to become a Notary in the state of New York. First, you must be 18 years of age or older. Second, you must be a New York resident or maintain an office or place of business in the state. And third, you must not have been convicted of a felony.

Although New York Executive Law, Section 130, states that an applicant must be a U.S. citizen, a 1984 U.S. Supreme Court decision, *Bernal v. Fainter*, holds that no state may deny a Notary commission merely because of a lack of U.S. citizenship. The website of the New York Department of State's Division of Licensing Services now stipulates, in the page covering frequently asked questions, that a Notary must be either a citizen or a permanent resident of the United States at the time of commissioning.

2. Obtain and study the *Notary Public License Law.*

If you are applying for a Notary commission for the first time, you must pass a written and proctored exam. This multiple-choice exam is based on the *Notary Public License Law* (NPLL), which is available on the website of the New York Department of State's Division of Licensing Services. At the time of this *Primer*'s publication, the URL for that site was http://www.dos.state.ny.us/lcns/lawbooks/notary.html. You also may request a copy of the NPLL by calling (518) 474-4429 (customer service representatives are available Monday, Tuesday, Wednesday and Friday, 9:00 a.m. to 1:00 p.m. and 2:00 p.m. to 4:45 p.m.), by emailing licensing@dos.ny.us, by writing the Department of State, Division of Licensing Services, P.O. Box 22001, Albany, NY 12201-2001, or by visiting the Division

3

in the Alfred E. Smith Office Building at 80 South Swan Street (10th Floor), Monday through Friday between 9:00 a.m. and 4:45 p.m.

You should study the NPLL thoroughly before taking the exam. It is also helpful to review the "Notary Laws Explained" chapter in this *Primer*, starting on page 21.

First-time applicants who are either current members of the New York State Bar Association or court clerks of the Unified Court System who were appointed to their positions after taking the relevant Civil Service exam are exempt from the exam but must complete all other requirements.

Notaries seeking to renew their commissions and former New York Notaries whose commissions expired less than six months ago also are exempt from taking the exam. However, they still must submit an application for reappointment.

3. Find the next available exam in your area.

Exams are administered at designated sites throughout New York. Exam schedules and complete instructions are posted on the website of the Division of Licensing Services. At the time of this *Primer*'s publication, the URL for that site was http://www. dos.state.ny.us/lcns/professions/notary/notary1.htm.

Exams are given regularly in the following cities: Albany, Binghamton, Buffalo, Franklin Square, Hauppauge, Newburgh, New York City, Plattsburgh, Rochester, Syracuse, Utica and Watertown. Exams are administered at state office buildings and other designated sites.

4. Take the exam.

Since there is no preregistration or guarantee of space, applicants should report to the selected site at least 15 minutes before the scheduled starting time of the exam. The policy is first-come, first-served.

Be prepared to present valid identification bearing your photo and signature (a New York driver's license, a nondriver's ID, a U.S. passport, military ID, USCIS-issued ID or a certificate of U.S. citizenship) and the nonrefundable exam fee of $15, which you may pay by Visa, MasterCard or check or money order payable to "New York Department of State" (cash will not be accepted). Applicants also must be thumbprinted prior to taking the exam. Any applicants who have been designated by a county clerk to serve the public at no charge are exempted from the exam fee but must meet all other requirements.

You will be given 60 minutes to complete the exam. You must answer at least 70 percent of the questions correctly in order to pass. Study and reference materials may not be used during the exam.

You will be notified by mail as soon as your exam results are available. Scores will not be discussed over the phone. If you pass the exam, be sure to keep your exam slip, as you must submit it with your application. If you fail, you may retake the exam at any time.

5. Obtain a commission application.

Once you have passed the Notary exam, you will be mailed an application form. The application is not available on the website.

If you are exempt from the exam, you may request an application form from the Division of Licensing Services by emailing licensing@dos.ny.us, by calling (518) 474-4429 or by writing or visiting the Division at the addresses already given above. Be sure to include your full name and mailing address when requesting an application. Forms may also be available at select Department of State or county clerks' offices; contact your local office(s) to confirm availability. (See pages 118–121 for contact information.)

6. Complete the application.

Follow the clear instructions on the reverse side of the application and complete the application in ink. On the application, you may not use a post office box as an address. A married woman must use her own name, not that of her spouse (for example, "Jane Smith," not "Mrs. John Smith"). Any false statements or omission of any information required by this form is cause for denial of a Notary commission.

Sign and date the form, then take the completed application to a commissioned Notary Public. He or she will administer your required oath of office.

7. File your exam results, application and oath of office.

Within two years after you pass the exam, you must mail your signed and notarized application, your original exam slip (not a copy) and a nonrefundable $60 fee to the Department of State's Division of Licensing Services at the postal address given above. Failure to file within two years will invalidate the results of the exam. If your application is approved, the Secretary of State will send your Notary commission directly to the clerk of the county in which you were commissioned, along with a copy of your oath of office and official signature for the clerk to keep on file.

Notaries seeking reappointment must submit their applications and the nonrefundable $60 fee to the local county clerk, not the Division of Licensing Services. For renewing Notaries, the commission is issued by the county clerk and remains on file in the clerk's office, along with your oath of office and official signature.

If your application is approved, the Department of State will send you an identification card stating your name, address and county of commissioning and the effective and expiration dates of your four-year commission. ■

Tools
of the Trade

There are several tools that Notaries need in order to carry out their duties lawfully and efficiently. These tools are as important to the Notary as a hammer and saw are to the carpenter.

Inking Stamp

Although not required by New York law, an inked stamp may be convenient to imprint certain required data on the document. The following information must be typed, printed or stamped on each notarial certificate: the Notary's name, the words "Notary Public State of New York," the name of the county in which the Notary originally qualified, the Notary's commission expiration date and, if applicable, the name of any county in which the Notary's certificate of official character has been filed, using the words "Certificate filed in _____ County."

Seal Embosser

While not required by New York law, the seal embosser is used in many states and is often vital on documents sent abroad. Many Notaries opt to affix an embossment in addition to an inked stamp. The seal embosser makes a non-photographically reproducible indentation on the document. Because photocopies of documents can easily pass as originals, the embossment can be used to distinguish an original from a photocopy. Also, embossing all pages in a document together can safeguard against later substitution or addition of pages.

Journal of Notarial Acts

New York law does not require Notaries to keep journals, but many lawsuits may be prevented if Notaries can demonstrate, through detailed and accurate journal records, that they have exercised reasonable care in executing their notarial acts. The journal should include the date, time and type of each official act; the date and type of document notarized; the signature and printed name and address of each person whose signature is notarized; the method used to identify the signer(s); and the fee charged for the notarization, if any.

Jurat Stamp

The jurat stamp impresses on an affidavit the jurat wording "Subscribed and sworn to before me this _____ day of _____, _____, by _____." The jurat stamp is more convenient (and safer, since critical wording will not be omitted) than typing or printing the wording on each affidavit that requires it.

Venue Stamp

A venue stamp impresses on a document the location of the notarization in the form, "State of _____, County of _____." A venue stamp may be used for acknowledgments, jurats or any other notarial act when otherwise acceptable notarial certificate wording does not include a venue statement.

Fingerprinting Device

Although New York law does not require a signer to affix a thumbprint in the Notary's journal, Notaries increasingly are asking signers to do so. A thumbprint serves as proof that a particular signer did or did not appear, thereby deterring fraud. Many Notaries opt for the convenience of an inexpensive inkless device that allows a thumbprint to be taken quickly and efficiently.

Notarial Certificates

The notarial certificate contains the required wording that, when completed by a commissioned Notary, states the facts certified by a Notary in a particular notarization. Occasionally a document will have no notarial wording, the provided wording will not meet the state's requirements or there will be no room for the Notary's seal. Preprinted notarial certificates for acknowledgments, jurats, proofs of execution by a subscribing witness and copy certification by a document custodian are available.

Errors and Omissions Insurance

Notary errors and omissions (E&O) insurance provides protection for Notaries who are sued for damages resulting from unintentional notarial mistakes. In the event of a lawsuit, the E&O insurance company will provide and pay for the Notary's legal counsel and absorb any damages levied by a court or agreed to in a settlement, up to the coverage limit. E&O insurance does not cover the Notary for intentional misconduct. ■

As a full-service organization, the National Notary Association makes available to New York Notaries all notarial items required by law, custom and convenience.

10 Most-Asked Questions

Every Notary has a question or two about whether and how to notarize. But there are certain questions that pop up again and again. These top 10 questions are asked repeatedly at the National Notary Association's seminars, at its annual National Conference of Notaries Public and through its Notary Information Service Hotline.

As with most questions about notarization, the answers to these 10 are not always a simple yes or no. Sometimes the answer is, "It depends."

1. May I notarize a will?

It depends. A Notary should notarize a will only if clear instructions and a notarial certificate are provided. If the signer of the will is relying on the Notary for advice on how to proceed, the Notary should tell the individual to consult with an attorney.

Laws regarding wills differ from state to state. Some states do not require notarization of wills, while others allow it as one of several witnessing options. Often it is not the signature on the will itself that is notarized, but the signatures of witnesses on affidavits appended to the will. That type of will is called a self-proving will, and New York Notaries may notarize the signatures of witnesses on such a will. (See "Self-Proving Wills," pages 64–65.)

The danger in notarizing wills is that would-be testators who have drafted their own wills without legal advice may believe that notarization will make their wills legal and valid. However, even when notarized, such homemade wills may be worthless because the testators failed to obtain the proper number of witnesses or omitted important information.

In fact, notarization itself may actually void an otherwise properly executed handwritten (holographic) will, because courts have occasionally held that any writing on the document other than the testator's invalidates the will.

2. May I notarize for a stranger with no identification?

Yes. If identification of a signer cannot be based on personal knowledge or identification documents (ID cards), a Notary may rely on the oath or affirmation of a personally known credible witness to identify an unknown signer.

The Notary must personally know the credible identifying witness, who must personally know the document signer. This establishes a chain of personal knowledge from the Notary through the credible identifying witness to the signer.

A credible identifying witness should be someone the Notary believes to be trustworthy and impartial. If a person has a financial or other beneficial interest in a document, that individual cannot be a reliably impartial witness.

When no credible identifying witness is available to identify a stranger with no IDs, the Notary may have no choice but to refer the signer to a personally known Notary or to a friend who personally knows a Notary.

3. May I notarize a photograph?

No. To simply affix a signature and seal on a photograph is improper. A Notary's signature and seal must appear only on a notarial certificate (such as an acknowledgment or jurat) accompanying a written statement signed by another person.

However, an individual's signature on a written statement referring to an accompanying or attached photograph may be notarized. If the photograph is large enough, the statement and notarial certificate might appear on its reverse side. Such a format might be acceptable when "notarized" photos are requested by persons seeking medical or health licenses or by legal residents renewing foreign passports.

A word of caution here: A Notary should always hesitate to notarize a photo-bearing card or document that could be used as a bogus "official" ID.

4. Is there a recommended practice to follow if there's no room for my seal or if it smears?

Yes. If there is not enough room on a document for the Notary's seal and signature, then the Notary should complete and attach a loose certificate, a separate sheet of paper containing the notarial wording, seal and signature. The Notary should neatly print or type on the document that a loose certificate is attached and should print or type on the loose certificate the particulars of the document to which it is attached.

If an initial seal impression is unreadable and there is room on the document, the Notary may affix another impression nearby. The illegibility of the first seal impression will indicate why a second impression was necessary. The Notary should record in the journal that a second impression was applied. If there is no room for a second seal impression, then the Notary should complete and attach a loose certificate, following the procedure described above.

A Notary should never attempt to fix an imperfect seal impression with a pen or correction fluid or both. This may be viewed as evidence of tampering and could cause the document to be rejected by a receiving agency.

5. May I notarize signatures on faxes or photocopies of documents?

It depends. If a photocopy or fax was signed with pen and ink, the signature may be notarized. But a signature that was photocopied or faxed may never be notarized, because it is impossible to determine the validity of such a signature. It is far too easy to cut a signature off one document, fraudulently paste it onto another document and then obliterate the evidence of the fraud by photocopying or faxing the altered document.

Notaries should be aware that sometimes public recorders will not accept notarized photocopies or faxes, even if the signatures are original, because the text of the documents may be too faint to adequately reproduce in microfilming.

6. May I notarize for customers only?

No. As a public official, a Notary is commissioned to notarize for anyone who reasonably requests service, not just the customers or clients of any one business. Even when a Notary's employer has paid for the commissioning fees and notarial supplies, the Notary's duty is to serve all members of the public without discriminating. There is no such officer as a "Notary Private."

It is ethically improper — although hardly ever explicitly prohibited by statute — to discriminate between customers and noncustomers in offering or refusing to offer notarial services and in charging or not charging fees.

Discrimination against anyone who presents a lawful request for notarization is not a suitable policy for a public official commissioned to serve all of the public equally. Also, laws prohibiting discrimination may be applicable and can provide the basis for lawsuits.

7. May I notarize a document in a language I can't read?

In most instances, yes. As long as the notarial certificate and document signature are in a language the Notary can read, New York Notaries are not expressly prohibited from notarizing documents written in languages they cannot read. If the certificate is in a language the Notary cannot read, then the Notary must add and complete the appropriate notarial wording in English.

There are, however, certain difficulties and dangers in notarizing documents that the Notary cannot read. The main difficulty for the Notary is making an accurate journal description of an unreadable document; the main danger to the public and the Notary is that the Notary has no way of determining whether the document is legitimate or fraudulent. As a result, the Notary might not be able to prevent a fraud from occurring and might even unknowingly perform an illegal act.

Under no circumstances should a notarization be performed if the Notary and the principal signer cannot communicate in the same language.

8. May I certify a copy of a birth certificate?

No. Some states — although not New York — allow Notaries to certify copies, but copies of either public records or documents that are publicly recordable should never be certified by Notaries. Only a county recording official should certify a copy of a deed or other recordable instrument, and only an officer in a Bureau of Vital Statistics should certify a copy of a birth certificate or other vital public record. A Notary's "certification" of a birth or death record may actually lend credibility to a counterfeit or altered document.

In states allowing Notary-certified copies, Notaries may properly certify copies only of documents privately held by individuals or entities, including personal papers, letters, college diplomas and in-house business documents.

9. Does a document have to be signed in my presence?

It depends. Documents requiring acknowledgments normally do not need to be signed in the Notary's presence. When performing an acknowledgment, the Notary certifies only that the signer of the document personally appeared before the Notary at the time of the notarization, was identified by the Notary and acknowledged (declared or stated) to the Notary that he or she freely signed for the purposes stated in the document.

On the other hand, documents requiring a jurat typically must be signed in the Notary's presence, as dictated by the typical jurat wording, "Subscribed and sworn to (or affirmed) before me...." However, if a jurat certificate merely reads, "Sworn to (or affirmed) before me ...," then the signature need not be affixed in the Notary's presence.

When performing a jurat, the Notary typically certifies that the signer personally appeared before the Notary, was given an oath or affirmation by the Notary and, usually, signed the document in the Notary's presence. In addition, even though the Notary may not be required by law to positively identify the signer for a jurat, it is always a good idea to do so.

10. May I notarize for a family member?

Yes and no. Although New York law does not prohibit notarizing for family members, Notaries who do so may violate the statutes prohibiting a direct beneficial interest — especially in notarizing a spouse's signature on a document that will be recorded in a state with community-property laws.

Besides the possibility of a financial interest in notarizing for a relative, there may be an emotional interest that can prevent the Notary from acting impartially. For example, a Notary who is asked to notarize a contract signed by his brother might attempt to persuade the sibling to sign or not sign. As a brother, the individual is entitled to exert influence; for a Notary, this is entirely improper.

Even if a Notary has no direct beneficial interest in the document and does not attempt to influence the signer, notarizing for a relative could subject the document to a legal challenge if other parties to the transaction allege that the Notary could not have acted impartially. ■

Steps to Proper Notarization

When Notaries perform a notarial act, they are expected to exercise what is known as "reasonable care." Reasonable care is the level of attentiveness and precaution expected of a person of ordinary intelligence. The first rule of reasonable care is strict adherence to all laws governing Notaries and notarization. In situations not explicitly covered by statute, a Notary should make every effort to use common sense and behave in a responsible and ethical fashion, following the accepted best practices for that situation.

A Notary should exercise reasonable care not only because failure to do so may result in disciplinary measures or a lawsuit to recover financial damages caused by an error, but also because the Notary's actions may facilitate a fraud that harms the very members of the public whom the Notary have been commissioned to protect. If, on the other hand, a Notary can convincingly show that he or she used reasonable care when performing a notarization, the public will be protected and the Notary will be shielded from liability in the event that the notarization is challenged.

The following 14-step checklist will help Notaries to apply the principles of reasonable care.

1. Require every signer to personally appear.

The signer must appear in person before the Notary on the date and in the county stated in the notarial certificate. "Personal appearance" means that the signer is in the Notary's physical presence — face to face in the same room. Communication between the Notary and the signer cannot be established over the phone, from another room, through the mail or through a third person.

2. Visually scan the document.

Notaries are not required to read the documents they notarize, and they are not responsible for the accuracy of the contents. However, they should note certain important particulars about a document — such as its title, date and number of pages — for recording in the journal of notarial acts. Notaries should count and record the number of pages. This can show whether pages are later fraudulently added or removed.

3. Look for blank spaces.

Documents with blank spaces have a great potential for fraudulent misuse. A borrower, for example, might sign an incomplete promissory note, trusting the lender to fill in the amount borrowed, only to discover later that the lender has written in an amount larger than what was actually borrowed.

The document signer should fill in any spaces left in the document. If the blanks are inapplicable and intended to be left unfilled, the signer should be asked to line through each space (using ink) or to write in "Not Applicable" or "N/A." If the signer does not know how the blanks should be filled in, then the Notary should ask him or her to contact the document's issuing agency.

4. Check the document's date.

For acknowledgments, the date of signing on the document must either precede or be the same as the date of the notarization; it may not follow it. A document whose signature date follows the date on its notarial certificate risks rejection by a recorder or other intended recipient, who may question how the signature could have been notarized before it was placed on the document. For a jurat, the document signing date and the notarization date are typically the same.

5. Make a careful identification.

The Notary should identify every document signer either through personal knowledge, reliable identification documents (ID cards) or the oath of a personally known credible identifying witness.

When using ID cards, the Notary must examine them closely to detect alteration, counterfeiting or evidence that they are issued to an impostor. Notaries should not rely on a type of card with which they are unfamiliar, unless they check it against a reference such as the *U.S. Identification Manual* or the *ID Checking Guide*.

6. Verify that the signer understands the document and is signing it voluntarily.

A conscientious and careful Notary will be certain not only of the signer's identity, but also of the signer's ability to understand the document and his or her willingness to sign it. It is in the best interest of both the Notary and the public for the Notary to make a commonsense judgment about these issues, because notarizing for someone who does not understand the consequences of the transaction or who has been coerced into signing may allow a fraud to occur.

Determining that a signature is a voluntary act — that is, freely made, without duress or undue influence — is relatively easy. The Notary simply asks the signer if he or she has signed or is about to sign the document willingly and then carefully watches for any indications to the contrary. If the Notary suspects that a signer is being forced or coerced into signing against his or her will, then the Notary should refuse to perform the notarization.

The Notary can establish a signer's awareness, or basic ability to understand what he or she is signing, by asking the signer simple questions about the document. If the signer cannot respond intelligibly to these questions, then the Notary may assume that the signer is not competent to sign at that moment. If a Notary is unsure of a signer's awareness, then the Notary may refuse service.

7. Check all signatures.

The various signatures the Notary will witness or examine during a notarization present opportunities to detect a forgery. When the signer signs the journal, the Notary should observe whether the signer appears to be laboring over the signature — a possible indication of a forgery in progress. The Notary also should compare the signature on the document with the signature in the journal. If the signer presents an identification document, then the Notary should compare the signature on the ID with the signatures on the document and in the journal.

When a document signer's identity is established by means of an ID card, the Notary must make sure that the signer signs the same name on the document as appears on the identification presented. Generally, a document signature that is a shorter form of the name on the ID card is acceptable. The signature may never be a longer form of the name on the ID. For example, a signer whose ID says John David Smith could sign as John D.

Smith, but if the signer's ID says John D. Smith, then he could not sign as John David Smith.

8. Keep a journal of notarial acts.

Although maintaining a journal of notarizations is not a statutory requirement in New York, many Notaries find that keeping a record of their official acts is a good business practice and a benefit to the people they serve. If a notarized document is lost or altered, or if certain facts about the transaction are later challenged, the Notary's journal becomes valuable evidence. It can protect the rights of all parties to a transaction and help Notaries defend themselves against false accusations.

The Notary should record all of the pertinent details of each notarization in the journal: the date, time and type of notarization; the date and type of document; the signature and printed name and address of each document signer and witness; the means by which each person was identified; and the notarial fees charged, if any. Any other pertinent data, such as any representative capacity the signer is claiming, also should be recorded. As a further deterrent to fraud, the Notary may ask the signer to leave a thumbprint in the journal.

9. Complete the journal entry first.

The Notary should complete the journal entry entirely before filling out the notarial certificate. This prevents a signer from leaving before the important public record of the notarization is made in the journal.

10. Make sure the document has notarial wording.

If a notarial certificate does not come with the document, the Notary must ask the document signer what type of notarization — acknowledgment or jurat, for example — is required. The Notary may then neatly print or type the appropriate notarial wording on the document or attach a preprinted loose certificate.

If the signer does not know what type of notarization is required, he or she should contact the document's issuing or receiving agency to determine this. This decision is never the Notary's to make unless the Notary is also an attorney.

11. Be attentive to details.

When completing the notarial certificate, the Notary needs to make sure that the venue statement is present and that it correctly identifies the place of notarization. If the venue statement is missing, the Notary must add it, either by hand or with a venue stamp. If the venue is preprinted and incorrect, the Notary either should line through the incorrect state and/or county and then neatly print the proper information or should cross out the entire venue statement and then replace it using an inked venue stamp. In either case, the Notary should initial and date the change.

Also, the Notary should pay attention to any text on the notarial certificate that indicates the number and gender of the document signers, as well as how they were identified. The Notary should line through or cross out any inapplicable text — for example, plurals and pronouns that do not apply to the signer(s) in question.

12. Affix your signature and seal properly.

A Notary should sign exactly the same name as that appearing on his or her commission. If a Notary uses an official seal, the seal impression should be placed as close to the Notary's signature as possible without overprinting it. To prevent illegibility, Notaries should not place their seals or signatures over printed material or a document signer's signature. Although an embossment may be placed over the letters "L.S." on a notarial certificate, an inking seal should be affixed next to but not over the letters to ensure legibility of the data in the seal.

New York and several other states do not require Notaries to use seals. However, New York Notaries must write, type or stamp certain required wording on the certificate.

13. Protect loose certificates.

If the Notary has to attach a notarial certificate, it should be securely stapled to the document's signature page. Notaries can protect against the fraudulent removal of an attached certificate by embossing it together with the document, by neatly printing or typing on the document that a loose certificate is attached and/or by neatly printing or typing on the loose certificate the particulars of the document to which the certificate is attached. For example, the following notation written on a loose certificate would deter its removal and fraudulent reattachment to another document: "This certificate is attached to a 15-page partnership agreement between John Smith and Mary Doe, signed December 14, 2010."

14. Don't give advice.

Every state prohibits nonattorneys from practicing law. A Notary should never choose the type of certificate or notarization that a document needs, prepare or complete documents for others or give advice on any matter relating to a document unless the Notary is an attorney or a professional certified or licensed in a relevant area of expertise. These decisions can have important legal ramifications, and the Notary could be held liable for any damages resulting from an incorrectly chosen certificate, notarization or document wording. ■

Notary Laws Explained

In layperson's language, this chapter discusses and clarifies key parts of the current laws of New York that regulate Notaries Public, as compiled by the New York Department of State (DOS) in the *Notary Public License Law* (NPLL), which is reprinted starting on page 85.

THE NOTARY COMMISSION

Qualifications for Commission

Qualifications. To become a Notary in New York, the applicant must:

1) Be at least 18 years old.

2) Be a resident of New York or maintain a place of business or office in the state (Executive Law § 130).

3) Complete and pass the New York State Notary Public exam (NPLL, "Introduction").

Citizenship. Although New York Executive Law, Section 130, states that an applicant must be a U.S. citizen, a 1984 Supreme Court decision, *Bernal v. Fainter*, declared that no state may deny a Notary commission merely because of a lack of U.S. citizenship. The New York Department of State's Division of Licensing Services (DLS) now stipulates that a Notary must be either a citizen or a permanent resident of the United States at the time of commissioning (DOS DLS website, "Notary Public: Frequently Asked Questions").

Disqualifications for Commission. The Department of State may reject an application for:

1) A conviction for a felony or certain other crimes, including using or carrying a firearm, buying or receiving stolen property, unlawful entry, drug-related offenses and prostitution (Executive Law § 130).

2) Removal from office as a commissioner of deeds for the city of New York (Executive Law § 140).

3) Violation of the Selective Draft Act of 1917, of the Selective Training and Service Act of 1940 or of subsequent amending or supplementing acts (Public Officers Law § 3).

4) Substantial and material misstatement or omission in the commission application (NPLL, "Restrictions and Violations: Executive Law").

May Not Be a Sheriff. Because sheriffs are barred from holding another public office, they may not be commissioned as Notaries Public (New York Constitution, Article XIII § 13-a).

Proctored Exam

Required. All first-time Notary applicants — and previously commissioned applicants whose commissions have lapsed for more than six months — must complete and pass a proctored, written exam prescribed by the Department of State's Division of Licensing Services (NPLL, "Introduction"). The exam is designed to satisfy the Secretary of State that applicants for a New York Notary commission are familiar with the duties and responsibilities of the office (Executive Law § 130).

The exam consists of multiple-choice questions on the terms and information in the NPLL. A score of 70 percent is required to pass the exam (DOS DLS website, "Notary Public: Exam Information and Schedule").

Exemptions. Current Notaries seeking to renew their commissions, former New York Notaries whose commissions have expired no more than six months prior to application, attorneys admitted to practice law in New York and court clerks of the Unified Court System who were appointed to their positions after taking the relevant Civil Service exam are exempt from the Notary exam (Executive Law § 130).

Thumbprints. All New York Notary applicants who are required to take the Notary exam will be thumbprinted at the testing site before they take the exam (DOS DLS website, "Notary Public: Exam Information and Schedule").

Exam Fee. A nonrefundable fee of $15 is payable when the exam is taken (DOS DLS website, "Notary Public: Exam Information and Schedule").

Application for Commission

Application Form. The application form will be mailed to the applicant after he or she has passed the Notary exam (DOS DLS website, "Notary Public"). Applications should be completed in ink.

Oath of Office. Applicants for a New York Notary commission must take their completed application to a commissioned Notary, who will administer the required oath of office and notarize the application form (Executive Law § 131 and NPLL, "Introduction").

The Notary administering the oath to the Notary applicant may not charge a fee (Public Officers Law § 69).

Application Submission. First-time applicants for a New York Notary commission must submit their original signed and notarized application to the Department of State's Division of Licensing Services (Executive Law § 131 and NPLL, "Introduction"). The application must be accompanied by the original exam slip indicating the applicant has passed the mandatory exam (NPLL, "Introduction"). All application materials must be submitted within two years of the exam date or the exam results will be invalid (DOS DLS website, "Notary Public: Exam Information and Schedule").

Application Fee. A nonrefundable $60 application fee must be submitted with the application (Executive Law § 131 and NPLL, "Introduction").

Commission Issuance and Filing

Approval. Once a commission application has been approved, the Secretary of State sends the Notary's commission and a copy of his or her oath of office and official signature to the clerk of the county in which the Notary was commissioned. For New York residents, this will be their county of residence; for nonresidents who maintain an office or place of business in the state, it will be the county where the office or business is located. The county clerk keeps the Notary's commission, oath and signature on file (Executive Law § 131 and NPLL, "Introduction").

Identification Card. Once a commission application has been approved, the Department of State sends the Notary an identification card stating his or her name, address and county of commissioning and the effective and expiration dates of the Notary's four-year commission (Executive Law § 131).

Notary Bond

Not Required. New York Notaries are not required to obtain a surety bond.

Liable for All Damages. Notaries have unlimited financial liability for any and all damages caused by their mistakes or misconduct in performing notarial acts. If a person is financially injured by a Notary's negligence or failure to properly perform a notarial act, whether intentional or unintentional, the injured party may sue the Notary in civil court. The Notary may be ordered to pay all resulting damages, including attorney's fees (Executive Law § 135).

Jurisdiction

Statewide. New York Notaries may perform official acts throughout the state of New York. They are not limited to the county or counties in which they live or work (Executive Law § 130).

New York Notaries may not notarize beyond the state borders. The Notary may not, for example, witness a signing outside of New York and then return to the state to perform the notarization. All parts of a given notarization must be performed at the same time and place within the state of New York.

Qualification as a Connecticut Notary. Residents of New York who maintain or are regularly employed in an office in Connecticut may qualify for a Connecticut Notary commission. For more information, write the Office of the Secretary of the State, Attn: LEAD/Notary Public Area, P.O. Box 150470, Hartford, CT 06115-0470, or call (860) 509-6232.

Qualification as a New Jersey Notary. Residents of New York who maintain or are regularly employed in an office in New Jersey may qualify for a New Jersey Notary commission. For more information, write the New Jersey Department of Treasury, Division of Revenue, Notary Public Unit, P.O. Box 452, Trenton, NJ 08646, or call (609) 292-9292.

Term of Office

Four-Year Term. The term of office for a New York Notary Public is four years (Executive Law § 130 and NPLL, "Introduction"). Each term begins with the date specified by the Department of State and ends at midnight on the commission expiration date.

Reappointment

Application Procedure. Notaries seeking reappointment must submit their signed application, notarized oath of office and nonrefundable $60 fee to the county clerk in the county in which they were commissioned, rather than to the Department of State (Executive Law § 131 and NPLL, "Introduction"). If the Notary applies for reappointment prior to or within six months of the expiration date of his or her current term, then no exam is required for reappointment (Executive Law § 130).

The application may be requested by emailing licensing@ dos.ny.us, by calling (518) 474-4429 or by writing or visiting the Division of Licensing Services in Albany. Forms also may be available at select other Department of State offices or county clerks' offices (DOS website, "Contact and Ordering Information").

Commission Issuance and Filing. For renewing Notaries, the commission is issued by the county clerk and remains on file in the clerk's office, along with the Notary's oath of office and official signature. Once the application for reappointment is approved, the Department of State sends the Notary an identification card stating his or her name, address and county of commissioning and the effective and expiration dates of the Notary's new four-year commission (Executive Law § 131).

Resignation

Procedure. To resign, a Notary should submit a written notice to the Department of State, giving an effective date. Resignation is appropriate if the Notary moves and does not retain a place of business or office in New York. It is recommended that the notice be sent by certified mail.

The resignation notice may also be sent to the office of the county clerk where the Notary was commissioned or has filed a certificate of official character.

If the resigning Notary has a seal of office or a stamp used to affix information on certificates, these should be destroyed or defaced to prevent fraudulent use.

Public-Employee Notaries

Appointment by County Clerk. Each county clerk is required to designate at least one member of his or her staff to act as a Notary Public. The Notary will be available in each county clerk's office to notarize documents for the public during normal business hours (County Law § 534).

Commission and Exam Fees. Such public-employee designees will be exempt from the fees for the Notary exam and the commission application (County Law § 534).

Notary Fees. No fees may be collected for notarial acts performed by a public-employee Notary (County Law § 534).

Change of Address

Procedure. Because a Notary's qualification to act as a New York Notary could be affected by a change of address, the Department of State should be informed of any change in the address of the Notary's residence, office or place of business (Executive Law § 131).

Loss of Residence but Not Business Address. A New York Notary who moves his or her residence out of New York but still maintains a place of business or an office in the state may retain the Notary commission (Executive Law § 130).

Loss of Residence and Business Address. A non-resident New York Notary who ceases to maintain an office or place of business within the state vacates his or her office. A New York Notary who moves his or her residence out of state and who does not have a business address within the state also vacates the office (Executive Law § 130).

Fee. For a change of address, the Department of State charges a non-refundable administrative fee of $10. This fee will not be imposed when such a change is made on an application for reappointment (Executive Law § 131).

Change of Name

Procedure. If a Notary changes his or her name, the Notary may submit a change of personal name form to the New York Department of State. If the Notary prefers, he or she may make the change when the commission is renewed (Executive Law § 131). In either case, the Notary must provide proof of the change of name (DOS DLS website, "Notary Public: Frequently Asked Questions").

Change of Name by Marriage. When a Notary marries during a four-year term of office, the Notary may continue to use the maiden or original name in the official signature and seal. If the Notary elects to use the new married name, however, the Notary must continue to use the maiden or original name in the signature and seal but may add the new married name in parentheses after the signature.

Upon renewing, the Notary may then apply for a new commission using either the maiden or original name or the new married name. The Notary must then perform all notarial functions under the name selected (NPLL, "Definitions and General Terms: Signature of Notary Public").

Religious Name. If a person has taken and is known by a name given by a religious order, that individual may be appointed as a New York Notary Public and officiate as such using the given religious name (NPLL, "Definitions and General Terms: Signature of Notary Public").

Fee. For a change of name, the Department of State charges a non-refundable administrative fee of $10. This fee will not be imposed when such a change is made on an application for reappointment (Executive Law § 131) or if the change is the result of a change in marital status (DOS DLS website: "Notary Public: Frequently Asked Questions").

Duplicate ID Card

Procedure. If a Notary loses his or her identification card, or if the card is destroyed or damaged, the Notary may submit to the Secretary of State a request for a replacement card. The Secretary of State will issue a new card, which will have the word "duplicate" stamped across its face (Executive Law § 131).

Fee. For issuing a duplicate identification card, the Department of State charges a non-refundable administrative fee of $10.

OFFICIAL NOTARIAL ACTS

Authorized Acts

Notaries may perform the following official acts:

- Acknowledgments certify that a signer personally appeared before the Notary, was identified by the Notary and acknowledged freely signing the document (Executive Law § 135). (See pages 30–34.)

- Oaths and Affirmations are solemn promises to a Supreme Being (oath) or solemn promises on one's own personal honor (affirmation) (Executive Law § 135 and Public Officers Law § 10). (See pages 35–37.)

- Jurats, as found in affidavits and other sworn documents, certify that a signer personally appeared before the Notary, took an oath or affirmation from the Notary and, usually, signed in the Notary's presence (Executive Law § 135). (See pages 37–39.)

- Depositions certify that the spoken words of a witness were accurately taken down in writing, though this act is most often done by skilled court reporters (Executive Law § 135). (See pages 39–40.)

- Proofs of Execution certify that a subscribing witness personally appeared and swore to the Notary that another person, the principal, signed a document (Real Property Law § 304 and Executive Law § 135). (See pages 40–44.)

- Protests certify that a written promise to pay, such as a bill of exchange, was not honored (Executive Law § 135). (See page 44.)

- Safe Deposit Box Openings by a bank must be witnessed by a Notary (Banking Law § 335). (See pages 44–45.)

Unauthorized Acts

Certified Copies. A certified copy is a verified exact duplicate of an original document. A New York Notary is not expressly authorized by law to issue certified copies.

Requests for certified copies should be directed to the agency that holds or issued the original. For certified copies of birth, death or marriage certificates, and other vital records, the person requesting the copy should be referred to the Bureau of Vital Statistics (or the equivalent) in the state where the event occurred. (See "Bureaus of Vital Statistics," pages 122–126).

In states that do not authorize Notaries to certify copies, Notaries may notarize a signed, written declaration made by the owner or holder of a document that a copy is a true copy of the original. This process is commonly called "copy certification by document custodian" and may serve as an acceptable alternative to a Notary-certified copy. The receiving party determines if this alternative is acceptable. The requesting person, not the Notary, should provide the declaration and specify the notarial act to be performed if a notarial certificate is not already provided on the declaration. Notaries should be careful not to guide the process or to make any recommendations or claims concerning the legality or sufficiency of this alternative.

Marriages. New York Notaries have no authority to perform marriages unless they are also members of clergy or other officials given statutory power to perform marriages or to take the acknowledgment of parties and witnesses to a written contract of marriage (Domestic Relations Law § 11).

Disqualifying Interest. Although the NPLL only specifies that a Notary may not take his or her own acknowledgment, a Notary must never notarize his or her own signature. The Department of State also directs Notaries not to notarize if they are a party to or have a financial or beneficial interest in the transaction or to administer oaths or affirmations to themselves (NPLL, "Appointment and Qualifications: Miscellaneous: Notary Public — Disqualifications" and "Definitions and General Terms: Oath").

Telephone Notarizations. Performing notarizations (including acknowledgments and jurats) over the telephone is absolutely prohibited, and a Notary who does so is guilty of a misdemeanor. A document signer, oath-taker or affirmant must personally appear before the Notary, face to face and in the same room, at the time of the notarization, not before or after (NPLL, "Definitions and General Terms: Acknowledgment," "Definitions and General Terms: Oath" and "Professional Conduct").

In addition, notarization based upon a Notary's recognition of a signature or on the unsworn word of a third party, without the signer's appearance before the Notary, is prohibited.

Wills. Notaries may not draft wills or offer legal advice about wills. Such actions are considered to be the unauthorized practice of law and expose the Notary to the attendant penalties (NPLL, "Professional Conduct" and "Restrictions and Violations: Wills"). (See "Unauthorized Practice of Law," pages 60–61.)

However, if instructed to do so, the Notary may notarize the signatures of witnesses on an affidavit designed to make a will "self-proving." (See "Self-Proving Wills," page 63.)

Acknowledgments

Definition and Terms. An acknowledgment is a notarial act in which a document signer formally declares, in the presence of an authorized officer, that he or she signed a document as a voluntary act and deed (NPLL "Definitions and General Terms: Acknowledgment").

In discussing acknowledgments, it is important to use proper terms. A Notary takes or executes an acknowledgment, while a document signer makes or gives an acknowledgment.

Purpose. Acknowledgments are one of the most common forms of notarization. Notaries execute acknowledgments on a variety of important documents, including powers of attorney, loan documents and deeds or other documents affecting real property that will be publicly recorded by a county official (Executive Law § 135).

According to the NPLL, the purposes of the acknowledgment are not only to promote the security of land titles and prevent fraud in conveying real property but also to furnish proof of the proper execution of conveyances. Such proof allows a document to be submitted into evidence without further proof of its execution and to be made a recordable instrument (NPLL "Definitions and General Terms: Acknowledgment").

In executing an acknowledgment, a Notary certifies three things (Executive Law § 135):

1) The signer personally appeared before the Notary on the date and in the county indicated on the notarial certificate. (Notarization cannot be based upon a telephone call or on a Notary's familiarity with a signature.)

2) The Notary positively identified the signer through either personal knowledge or satisfactory evidence.

3) The signer acknowledged to the Notary that the signature was freely made for the purposes stated in the document. (If a document is willingly signed in the presence of the Notary, this act serves just as well as an oral statement of acknowledgment.)

Identification of Signer. In executing an acknowledgment, the Notary must identify the signer through personal knowledge or satisfactory evidence (Real Property Law § 303 and NPLL, "Professional Conduct" and "Definitions and General Terms: Acknowledgment"). Satisfactory evidence is defined as identification documents or a credible identifying witness. (See "Identifying Document Signers," pages 45–46.)

Procedure. The New York Department of State specifically prohibits Notaries from taking an acknowledgment over the telephone. The acknowledger must physically appear in front of the Notary (NPLL, "Professional Conduct" and "Definitions and General Terms: Acknowledgment").

For an acknowledgment, the document does not have to be signed in the Notary's presence. However, the signer must verbally acknowledge to the Notary that he or she willingly signed the document.

A document could have been signed an hour before, a week before, a year before, etc. — as long as the signer appears before the Notary with the signed document at the time of notarization to admit that the signature is his or her own.

Representative Capacity. Acknowledgments may be signed by a person acting in either an individual or a representative capacity, such as corporate officer, attorney in fact or partner.

If the uniform or all-purpose acknowledgment certificate prescribed by Section 309-a of New York's Real Property Law is used, the Notary Public need not ascertain that the signer holds the representative capacity claimed, since the form does not state the exact capacity of the signer. However, nothing prevents the careful Notary from asking a representative signer for documentary proof that he or she actually holds the capacity claimed. For an attorney in fact, this proof would be the power of attorney naming the attorney in fact as an agent for the principal; for a partner, it might be the written agreement that formed the partnership; and for a corporate officer, it might be the board of director's written order appointing the signer as a corporate agent. (A business card by itself does not constitute adequate documentary proof of a corporate agent's representative status.)

Because New York's all-purpose acknowledgment certificate does not state the signer's exact capacity, it is important that this capacity be explicitly stated somewhere on the notarized document or certificate. An attorney in fact, for example, might clarify whom he or she is representing by signing the document in the following or a similar manner: "Michael S. Jones, Attorney in Fact for Diane A. Jones, Principal."

Certificate for Acknowledgment. Upon taking the acknowledgment of any document signer, the Notary must complete an appropriate certificate of acknowledgment. The certificate wording will be printed either at the end of the document or on an attachment, called a loose certificate, which the Notary staples to the document's signature page (Real Property Law § 306).

Acknowledgment Certificate for New York Real Estate. New York statute prescribes a uniform or all-purpose acknowledgment certificate (below) which is adaptable for signers who are acknowledging a signature as an individual or in any representative capacity, such as partner and attorney in fact. This certificate — or any substantially similar form — must be used for all acknowledgments taken within New York on any document affecting real property located within the state, including those signed by corporate officers. No other acknowledgment certificate is authorized for New York Notaries notarizing real estate documents for property in the state (Real Property Law § 309-a).

State of New York   )

) ss.:

County of _____) .

On the _____ day of _____ in the year _____ before me, the undersigned, a Notary Public, personally appeared _____, personally known to me or proved to me on the basis of satisfactory evidence to be the individual(s) whose name(s) is (are) subscribed to the within instrument and acknowledged to me that he/she/they executed the same in his/her/their capacity(ies), and that by his/her/their signature(s) on the instrument, the individual(s), or the person upon behalf of which the individual(s) acted, executed the instrument.

_____ (Signature of Notary)

(Seal of Notary, if any)

(Other required data printed, typewritten or stamped)

For documents affecting New York real estate that are acknowledged before a Notary of another state, New York law provides an acknowledgment form whose use is optional for the out-of-state Notary (Real Property Law § 309-b).

Other Acknowledgment Certificates. For acknowledgments on documents not affecting New York real property, affecting real property in another state or not affecting real property at all, New York Notaries should use any other appropriate customary or statutory form, including the following two statutory certificates for signers representing a corporation. It must be reemphasized, however, that these two corporate acknowledgment certificates are prohibited on documents notarized in New York that affect New York real estate — but they, or a substantially similar certificate, must be used on all other documents signed and acknowledged in New York by a corporate representative (Real Property Law § 309).

State of New York   )

) ss.:

County of _____)

On the _____ day of _____ in the year _____ before me personally came _____, to me known, who, being by me duly sworn, did depose and say that he/she/they reside(s) in _____ (if the place of residence is in a city, include the street and street number, if any, thereof); that he/she/

they is (are) the (president or other officer or director or attorney in fact duly appointed) of the (name of corporation), the corporation described in and which executed the above instrument; that he/she/they know(s) the seal of said corporation; that the seal affixed to said instrument is such corporate seal; that it was so affixed by authority of the board of directors of said corporation, and that he/she/they signed his/her/their name(s) thereto by like authority.

_____ (Signature of Notary)

(Seal of Notary, if any)

(Other required data printed, typewritten or stamped)

State of New York   )
) ss.:
County of _____   )

On the ____ day of _____ in the year ____ before me personally came _____, to me known, who, being by me duly sworn, did depose and say that he/she/they reside(s) in _____ (if the place of residence is in a city, include the street and street number, if any, thereof); that he/she/they is (are) the (president or other officer or director or attorney in fact duly appointed) of the (name of corporation), the corporation described in and which executed the above instrument; and that he/she/they signed his/her/their name(s) thereto by authority of the board of directors of said corporation.

_____ (Signature of Notary)

(Seal of Notary, if any)

(Other required data printed, typewritten or stamped)

Who May Take. In addition to a Notary, the following officials may take, anywhere in the state, acknowledgments and proofs relating to real estate: a supreme-court justice, an official title examiner and an official referee.

Other officials — such as a court judge, a commissioner of deeds, a mayor, a city recorder, a surrogate or a county clerk — may take acknowledgments in their respective districts. Certain other town or village officials may also take acknowledgments in the towns or villages where they perform their official duties (Real Property Law § 298).

Married Women. A woman's marital status has no effect on her acknowledgment before a Notary. A Notary takes the acknowledgment made by a married woman in the same manner as if she were unmarried (Real Property Law § 302).

Oaths and Affirmations

Definition and Terms. An oath is a solemn, spoken pledge to a Supreme Being. An affirmation is a solemn, spoken pledge on one's own personal honor, with no reference to a Supreme Being. A person who objects to taking an oath may instead be given an affirmation. Both types of pledge are usually a promise of truthfulness or fidelity and have the same legal effect (NPLL, "Professional Conduct").

Purpose. The primary purpose of an oath or affirmation is to compel an individual to be truthful. This is done by appealing to the conscience of the oath-taker or affirmant and by arousing his or her fear of the potential ramifications of perjury (deliberately lying under oath or affirmation). In taking an oath or affirmation in an official proceeding, a person may be subject to criminal penalties should he or she fail to be truthful (NPLL, "Restrictions and Violations: Perjury").

An oath or affirmation can be part of the process of notarizing a document, as when executing a jurat or swearing in a credible identifying witness, or it can be a full-fledged notarial act in its own right, as when swearing in or administering an oath of office to a public official. New York Notaries may administer any oath required by state law, including oaths of office to public officials (Public Officers Law § 10).

For an oath or affirmation to be valid, the person swearing or affirming must do the following (NPLL, "Professional Conduct" and "Definitions and General Terms: Oath"):

1) Swear or affirm in the physical presence of the Notary.

2) Unequivocally swear or affirm that what is stated is true.

3) Swear or affirm as of that time.

4) Conscientiously take upon him- or herself the obligations of the oath or affirmation.

Procedure. The oath-taker or affirmant must physically appear in front of the Notary to take the oath or affirmation. The New York Department of State specifically prohibits Notaries from administering an oath or affirmation over the telephone. In addition, a Notary may not administer an oath or affirmation to him- or herself.

Because an oath or affirmation is a personal commitment of conscience that individuals can only make for themselves, no one may take an oath or affirmation on behalf of another person. In addition, an entity — such as a corporation or a partnership — may not take an oath or affirmation. However, a person representing a corporation, partnership or other legal entity may take an oath or affirmation as an individual, swearing that he or she has the authority to sign for the entity.

To impress upon the oath-taker or affirmant the importance of truthfulness, the Notary is encouraged to lend a sense of ceremony and formality to the oath or affirmation. During administration of the oath or affirmation, the Notary and the oath-taker or affirmant traditionally raise their right hands, though this is not a legal requirement. Notaries generally have discretion to use words and gestures they believe will most compellingly appeal to the conscience of the oath-taker or affiant (NPLL, "Professional Conduct" and "Definitions and General Terms: Oath").

Wording for Oath (Affirmation). If law does not dictate otherwise, a New York Notary may use the following or similar words in administering an oath or affirmation:

- Oath (Affirmation) for affiant signing an affidavit or deponent signing a deposition:

  Do you solemnly swear that the statements in this document are true to the best of your knowledge and belief, so help you God?

  (Do you solemnly, sincerely and truly declare and affirm that the statements in this document are true to the best of your knowledge and belief?)

- Oath (Affirmation) for credible identifying witness:

  Do you solemnly swear that you know this signer to be the person he/she claims to be, so help you God?

  (Do you solemnly, sincerely and truly declare and affirm that you know this signer to be the person he/she claims to be?)

- Oath (Affirmation) for subscribing witness:

  Do you solemnly swear that you saw (name of the document signer) sign his/her name to this document and/or that he/she acknowledged to you having executed it for the purposes therein stated, so help you God?

(Do you solemnly, sincerely and truly declare and affirm that you saw [name of document signer] sign his/her name to this document and/or that he/she acknowledged to you having executed it for the purposes therein stated?)

The person taking the oath or affirmation must respond by repeating these words in the first person ("I solemnly swear ...") or by answering affirmatively with "I do," "Yes" or similar words (NPLL, "Definitions and General Terms: Oath"). A nod or grunt is not a clear and sufficient response. If a person is mute and unable to speak, the Notary may rely upon written notes to communicate.

Jurats

Definition and Terms. A jurat is a notarial act in which a Notary certifies that a signer has, in the Notary's presence, voluntarily signed a document and taken an oath or affirmation vouching for the truthfulness of the signed document.

The NPLL further defines a jurat as that part of an affidavit where the Notary certifies that it (the affidavit) was sworn to or affirmed before the Notary (NPLL, "Definitions and General Terms: Jurat"). In other words, the term jurat can refer to the notarial act itself, or it can refer to the notarial certificate.

Purpose. Notaries typically execute a jurat when notarizing affidavits, depositions and other forms of written verification requiring a verbal oath or affirmation by the signer. The purpose of a jurat is to certify that the signer swore to or affirmed the truthfulness of statements in a document, which he or she usually signs in the Notary's presence. The oath or affirmation required for this notarial act compels the signer to be truthful by appealing to his or her conscience and by arousing his or her fear of criminal penalties for perjury.

In executing a jurat, a Notary certifies three things (Executive Law § 135):

1) The signer personally appeared before the Notary on the date and in the county indicated on the notarial certificate. (Notarization cannot be based upon a telephone call or on a Notary's familiarity with a signature).

2) The Notary watched the signature being made at the time of notarization, unless not stipulated by the jurat wording.

3) The Notary administered an oath or affirmation to the signer.

Identification of Signer. Even though identifying the signer is not required by New York law for jurats, the prudent Notary will always take pains to positively identify each signer, as is required by law for an acknowledgment. (See "Identifying Document Signers," pages 45–46.)

Procedure. As indicated above, a jurat normally requires an individual both to sign a document in the presence of the Notary and to swear or affirm that the contents of the document are true. The Notary then completes a notarial certificate that attests to those two facts. In such cases, if the document already has been signed, then the person must sign it again in front of the Notary.

A Notary Public does not execute a jurat merely by asking whether the signature on a document is that of the signer. A jurat always requires the person to take a verbal oath or affirmation attesting to the truthfulness of the contents of the document (NPLL, "Definitions and General Terms: Oath"). For this portion of a jurat, the Notary follows the standard procedure for administering an oath or affirmation.

Oath (Affirmation) for Jurat. If not otherwise prescribed by law, a Notary may use the following or similar words to administer an oath or affirmation in conjunction with a jurat:

> Do you solemnly swear that the statements in this document are true to the best of your knowledge and belief, so help you God?
>
> (Do you solemnly, sincerely and truly declare and affirm that the statements in this document are true to the best of your knowledge and belief?)

Certificate for Jurat. A typical jurat is the wording "Subscribed and sworn to (or affirmed) before me on this _____ (date) by _____ (name of signer)," or similar language. "Subscribed" means signed.

The NPLL, on the other hand, recommends as "generally employed" a form of jurat which certifies only that the signer took the oath or affirmation: "Sworn to before me this _____ day of _____ (month), _____ (year)" (NPLL, "Definitions and General Terms: Jurat"). This certificate wording indicates that the oath, not the signature, is the primary part of a jurat.

When jurat wording is not prescribed in a given instance, the National Notary Association recommends the following:

State of New York   )

) ss.:

County of _____   )

Subscribed and sworn to (or affirmed) before me this _____ day of _____ (month), _____ (year), by _____ (name of signer).

_____ (Signature of Notary)

                                        (Seal of Notary, if any)

(Other required data printed, typewritten or stamped)

Depositions and Affidavits

Definition and Terms. A deposition is a signed transcript of the signer's oral statements, taken down for use in a judicial proceeding. The deposition signer is usually called the deponent but may also be referred to as the affiant (NPLL, "Definitions and General Terms: Deponent" and "Definitions and General Terms: Deposition").

An affidavit is a statement that has been voluntarily signed and sworn to or affirmed before a Notary or other official with oath-administering powers. The affidavit signer is called an affiant (NPLL, "Definitions and General Terms: Affidavit").

Purpose. Depositions are used only in judicial proceedings. With a deposition, both sides in a lawsuit or court case have the opportunity to cross-examine the deponent. Questions and answers are transcribed into a written statement, and the deposition is then signed and sworn to before an oath-administering official (NPLL, "Definitions and General Terms: Deposition").

Affidavits are used in and out of court for a variety of purposes, from declaring losses to an insurance company to declaring U.S. citizenship before traveling to a foreign country. If the affidavit is used in a judicial proceeding, only one side in the case need participate in the execution of the affidavit, and cross-examination of the affiant is not allowed.

Procedure. New York Notaries have the power to take depositions, but this duty is most often executed by trained and certified shorthand reporters, also known as court reporters. While most Notaries do not have the stenographic skills necessary to transcribe a deponent's words, any Notary is competent to administer an oath or affirmation or to execute a jurat on an existing deposition (Executive Law § 135).

While Rule 3113 of the New York Civil Practice Law and Rules allows a Notary to take a deposition in a civil lawsuit, a deposition may not be taken on Sunday in such a civil proceeding. This rule, however, does not prohibit Notaries from otherwise administering oaths and affirmations and taking affidavits and acknowledgments on Sunday (NPLL, "Definitions and General Terms: Sunday").

In an affidavit, the Notary's certificate typically sandwiches the affiant's signed statement, with the venue and affiant's name at the top of the document and the jurat wording at the end. The Notary is responsible for accurately filling in the venue and the affiant's name and for any notarial text at the beginning and end of the affidavit. The affiant is responsible for the signed statement in the middle. The Notary also must administer an oath or affirmation, since the silent delivery to a Notary of a signed affidavit for certification of its accuracy is not sufficient (NPLL, "Definitions and General Terms: Affidavit").

<u>Oath (Affirmation) for Depositions and Affidavits</u>. If no other wording is prescribed in a given instance, a Notary may use the following language in administering an oath or affirmation for an affidavit or deposition (NPLL, "Professional Conduct"):

> Do you solemnly swear that the contents of this affidavit (or deposition) subscribed by you are correct and true to the best of your knowledge and belief, so help you God?

> (Do you solemnly, sincerely, and truly declare and affirm that the contents of this affidavit [or deposition] subscribed by you are correct and true to the best of your knowledge and belief?)

For both oath and affirmation, the affiant or deponent must respond aloud and affirmatively, with "I do" or similar words (NPLL, "Professional Conduct" and "Definitions and General Terms: Oath").

<u>Certificate for Deposition or Affidavit</u>. Depositions and affidavits require jurat certificates.

Proofs of Execution by Subscribing Witness

<u>Definition and Terms</u>. A proof of execution by subscribing witness is a notarial act that may be used in situations when a

signature on a document must be notarized but the person who signed the document, known as the principal signer or principal, is unable to personally appear before the Notary.

For a proof of execution, a person called the subscribing witness either watches (witnesses) the principal sign (execute) the document or takes the principal's acknowledgment of having signed. The subscribing witness then signs (subscribes) his or her own name on the document, at the principal's request and in the principal's presence. Finally, the subscribing witness brings that document to a Notary on the principal's behalf and verifies under oath or affirmation (proves) that he or she took the necessary steps to verify that the principal's signature is genuine and freely made.

Purpose. In executing a proof of execution by subscribing witness, a Notary certifies that the signature of a person who does not appear before the Notary — the principal — is genuine and freely made based upon the sworn testimony of another person who does appear — the subscribing witness.

Proofs of execution are used when the principal signer is out of town or otherwise unavailable to appear before a Notary. Because of their high potential for fraudulent abuse, proofs of execution are not universally accepted, though they are legal for the New York Notary to perform. Proofs should only be used as a last resort and never merely because the principal prefers not to take the time to personally appear before a Notary.

In performing a proof of execution, a Notary certifies three things:

1) The subscribing witness personally appeared before the Notary on the date and in the county indicated on the notarial certificate.

2) The Notary positively identified the subscribing witness through either personal knowledge or satisfactory evidence.

3) The Notary administered an oath or affirmation to the subscribing witness.

Identification of Witness. Since the Notary is relying entirely upon the word of the subscribing witness to vouch for an absent principal's identity, willingness and general competency, it is best for subscribing witnesses to be personally known to the

Notary. New York law, however, allows the Notary to identify a subscribing witness through satisfactory evidence (Real Property Law § 304). Satisfactory evidence of identity is established by means of identification documents or a credible identifying witness. (See "Identifying Document Signers," pages 45–46.)

Under New York law, the subscribing witness must personally know the principal (Real Property Law § 304). The ideal subscribing witness also should have no personal beneficial or financial interest in the document or transaction. It would be foolish of the Notary, for example, to rely upon the word of a subscribing witness who presents for notarization a power of attorney that names the same witness as attorney in fact.

Procedure. The subscribing witness must either watch the principal sign the document or take the principal's acknowledgment that he or she willingly signed the document at some earlier time. The principal then must ask the subscribing witness to affix his or her own signature to the document, as proof that he or she witnessed the principal's signature or took the principal's acknowledgment, and to take the signed document to a Notary.

The subscribing witness must personally appear before a Notary, who must identify him or her as the person who witnessed the signature or took the acknowledgment of the principal. The subscribing witness must state his or her place of residence and, if the witness's residence is in a city, the street and street number (Real Property Law § 304). Finally, the Notary must administer an oath or affirmation to the subscribing witness, who must swear or affirm that he or she personally knows the principal, that the principal's signature is genuine, that the principal willingly signed the document and that the principal requested the witness to also sign the document and bring it to a Notary (Real Property Law § 304 and NPLL, "Definitions and General Terms: Proof").

Oath (Affirmation) for Subscribing Witness. An acceptable oath for the subscribing witness might be:

> Do you solemnly swear that you know (name of document signer) to be the individual who executed this document, that you saw (name of document signer) sign his/her name to this document and/or that he/she acknowledged to you having executed it for the purposes therein stated, and that you signed your own name to the document as a witness thereto, so help you God?

(Do you solemnly, sincerely, and truly declare and affirm that you know [name of document signer] to be the individual who executed this document, that you saw [name of document signer] sign his/her name to this document and/or that he/she acknowledged to you having executed it for the purposes therein stated, and that you signed your own name to the document as a witness thereto?)

In Lieu of Acknowledgment.

On recordable documents, a proof of execution by a subscribing witness is usually regarded as an acceptable substitute for an acknowledgment.

New York law authorizes Notaries to execute proofs of execution in place of acknowledgments (Real Property Law § 304).

Certificate for Proof of Execution.

When executing a proof on a document affecting real property in New York, a Notary must use the following certificate, or a substantially similar form (Real Property Law § 309-a). Whatever form is used, it must state the place of residence of the subscribing witness (Real Property Law § 304):

State of New York   )

) ss.:

County of _____)

On the _____ day of _____ in the year _____ before me, the undersigned, personally appeared _____, the subscribing witness to the foregoing instrument, with whom I am personally acquainted, who, being by me duly sworn, did depose and say that he/she/they reside(s) in _____ (if the place of residence is in a city, include the street and street number, if any, thereof); that he/she/they know(s) _____ to be the individual described in and who executed the foregoing instrument; that said subscribing witness was present and saw said _____ execute the same; and that said witness at the same time subscribed his/her/their name(s) as a witness thereto.

_____ (Signature of Notary)

                         (Seal of Notary, if any)

(Other required data printed, typewritten or stamped)

For documents affecting New York real estate that are executed by proof of execution before a Notary Public of another state, New York statute provides a proof certificate whose use is optional for the out-of-state Notary (Real Property Law § 309-b).

When executing a proof on a document that does not affect

New York real property, affects real property in another state or does not affect real property at all, New York Notaries should use any other appropriate customary or statutory proof form. Any form used, however, must state the subscribing witness's residence address (Real Property Law § 306).

Protests

Definition and Terms. A protest is a written statement by a Notary or other authorized officer, verifying that payment was not received on a negotiable instrument such as a bill of exchange, bank draft or promissory note (NPLL, "Definitions and General Terms: Protest").

Before issuing a certificate of protest, the Notary must present the negotiable instrument to the person, firm or institution obligated to pay, a procedure called presentment. Failure to pay is called dishonor.

Purpose. While protests were common notarial acts in the United States in the 19th century, they are rarely performed today due to the advent of modern electronic communications and resulting changes in our banking and financial systems. Modern Notaries most often encounter protests in the context of international commerce.

Procedure. Notarial acts of protest are complicated and varied, requiring a special knowledge of financial and legal terminology. Only Notaries who have the requisite knowledge, or who are acting under the supervision of an experienced bank officer or an attorney familiar with the Uniform Commercial Code, should attempt a protest.

Witnessing Safe Deposit Box Opening

Definition and Terms. In this notarial act, the Notary, acting as an impartial witness, oversees the process of opening a safe deposit box and removing and cataloging its contents.

Purpose. When a Notary witnesses the opening and inventorying of a safe deposit box and then issues a certificate which clearly states the facts pertaining to the process, this protects the rights and interests of both the bank that provided the safe deposit box and the lessee whose personal property is stored in it.

In New York, witnessing the opening of a safe deposit box is a notarial act performed almost exclusively by Notaries employed by banks and other financial institutions.

Procedure. If the rental fee on a safe deposit box has not been paid, and at least 30 days have passed since the bank gave proper notice to the lessee and received no response, then the bank may open and inventory the contents of the box in the presence of a Notary Public.

The Notary then issues a certificate stating the lessee's name, the date the box was opened, the catalog of items removed from the box and any other relevant facts. Within 10 days of the box's opening, a copy of the certificate must be mailed by the lessor (the bank) to the lessee's last known address (Banking Law § 335).

Certificate for Inventorying a Safe Deposit Box. New York law does not provide specific wording for the certificate. The following wording is suggested:

State of New York   )
) ss.:
County of _____)

On the _____ (day) of _____ (month), _____ (year), safe deposit box number _____, rented in the name of _____, was opened by _____ (name of financial institution) in my presence and in the presence of _____ (name of financial institution officer). The contents of the box consisted of the following:

(list of contents)

_____ (Signature of financial institution officer)
_____ (Print or type name)
_____ (Signature of Notary)

                              (Seal of Notary, if any)
(Other required data printed, typewritten or stamped)

PRACTICES AND PROCEDURES

Identifying Document Signers

Identification for Acknowledgments. When a Notary takes the acknowledgment of a signature on any document, New York law requires the Notary to identify the acknowledger (Real Property

Law § 303). The following three methods of identification are acceptable:

1) The Notary's personal knowledge of the signer's identity (see "Personal Knowledge of Identity," pages 46–47)

2) Reliable identification documents or ID cards (see "Identification Documents [ID Cards]," pages 47–48)

3) The oath or affirmation of a personally known credible identifying witness (see "Credible Identifying Witness," pages 48–49)

Identification for Other Notarial Acts. While the law specifies identification standards only for acknowledgers, the prudent and conscientious Notary will apply these same standards in identifying any signer, whether for an acknowledgment, a jurat or any other notarial act.

Personal Knowledge of Identity

Definition. The safest and most reliable method of identifying a document signer is for the Notary to depend upon his or her own personal knowledge of the signer's identity. Personal knowledge means familiarity with an individual resulting from interactions with that person over a period of time sufficient to eliminate every reasonable doubt that the person has the identity claimed. The familiarity should come from association with the individual in relation to other people and should be based upon a chain of circumstances surrounding the individual.

New York law does not specify how long a Notary must be acquainted with an individual before personal knowledge of identity may be claimed, so the Notary's common sense must prevail. In general, the longer the Notary is acquainted with a person, and the more random interactions the Notary has had with that person, the more likely it is that the individual is personally known.

For instance, the Notary might safely regard a friend since childhood as personally known but would be foolish to consider a person met for the first time the previous day as such. Whenever the Notary has a reasonable doubt about a signer's identity, that individual should be considered not personally known and the identification should be made through satisfactory evidence (Real Property Law § 303). Satisfactory evidence consists either of reliable identification documents or of a credible identifying witness.

Identification Documents (ID Cards)

Acceptable ID Documents. Notaries customarily are allowed to use reliable identification documents (ID cards) to identify document signers whom they do not personally know. In lieu of personal knowledge, such cards are considered to be satisfactory evidence of identity.

The best ID cards have three components: a photograph, the signature and a physical description (e.g., height, weight, hair and eye color) of the bearer. Generally reliable forms of identification include:

- New York driver's license or official nondriver's ID

- U.S. and foreign passports

- U.S. military ID

- Permanent Resident ID, or "green card," issued by the United States Citizenship and Immigration Services (USCIS)

Multiple ID Documents. While one good identification document or card may be sufficient to identify a signer, the Notary may always ask for more.

Unacceptable ID Documents. Identification documents that are not acceptable for identifying acknowledgers include Social Security cards, credit cards, temporary driver's licenses, driver's licenses without photographs and birth certificates.

Fraudulent ID Documents. Identification documents are the least secure of the three methods of identifying a document signer because phony ID cards are common. The Notary should scrutinize each card for indications that the card has been altered, is a counterfeit or is a genuine card that has been issued to an impostor.

Some clues that an ID card may have been fraudulently altered include mismatched type styles, a photograph raised from the surface, a signature that does not match the signature on the document, unauthorized lamination of the card, smudges, erasures, smears and discolorations.

Possible tip-offs to a counterfeit ID card include misspelled words, a new-looking card with an old date of issuance, two cards with exactly the same photograph and inappropriate patterns and features.

Some possible indications that a card may have been issued to an impostor include a birth date or address that is unfamiliar to the bearer, ID cards that all seem brand new and a bearer who is unwilling to leave a thumbprint in the journal. (Such a print is not required by New York law but is requested by some Notaries as protection against forgeries, frauds and lawsuits.)

Credible Identifying Witness

Purpose. When a document signer is not personally known to the Notary and cannot produce an acceptable ID document, that signer may be identified on the oath or affirmation of a credible identifying witness. A credible identifying witness is generally regarded as a form of satisfactory evidence of identity that is equivalent to the Notary's personal knowledge of a signer's identity.

Identification of Witness. Every credible identifying witness must personally know the document signer. The credible identifying witness must also be personally known by the Notary. This establishes a chain of personal knowledge, from the Notary to the credible identifying witness to the signer. In a sense, a credible identifying witness is a walking, talking ID card.

Credible witnesses must never themselves be identified by the Notary through ID cards. Any credible identifying witness should have a reputation for honesty and should be a competent, independent individual who won't be tricked, cajoled, bullied or otherwise influenced into identifying someone he or she does not really know. In addition, the witness should have no personal interest in the transaction requiring a notarial act.

Oath (Affirmation) for Credible Identifying Witness. To ensure truthfulness, the Notary must administer an oath or affirmation to each credible identifying witness.

If not otherwise prescribed by New York law, an acceptable credible-witness oath or affirmation might be:

> Do you solemnly swear that you know this signer is the person he/she claims to be, so help you God?
>
> (Do you solemnly, sincerely, and truly declare and affirm that you know this signer is the person he/she claims to be?)

Procedure. If the Notary maintains a journal — although a journal is not required by New York law — a credible identifying witness and the document signer should sign the Notary's journal. The Notary should also print the witness's name and address in the journal.

Comparison to Subscribing Witness. Do not confuse credible identifying witnesses with subscribing witnesses. A credible identifying witness vouches for the identity of a signer who appears before the Notary. A subscribing witness vouches for the genuineness of the signature of a person who does not appear before the Notary. (See "Proof of Execution by Subscribing Witness," pages 40–44.)

Journal of Notarial Acts

Recommended. Although a journal is not required by law in New York, the National Notary Association and many Notary-regulating officials across the nation strongly recommend that every Notary keep a detailed, accurate and sequential journal of notarial acts.

Prudent Notaries keep detailed and accurate journals of their notarial acts for many reasons:

- Keeping records is a businesslike practice that every conscientious businessperson and public official should engage in. Not keeping records of important transactions, whether private or public, is risky.

- A Notary's journal protects the public's rights to valuable property and to due process by providing documentary evidence in the event a document is lost or altered or a transaction is later challenged.

- In the event of a civil lawsuit alleging that the Notary's negligence or misconduct caused the plaintiff serious financial harm, a detailed journal of notarial acts can protect the Notary by showing that reasonable care was used to identify a signer. For example, it would be difficult to contend that the Notary did not bother to identify a signer if the Notary's journal contained a detailed description of the ID card that the signer presented.

- Since civil lawsuits arising from a contested notarial act typically take place three to six years after the act occurs, the Notary cannot normally testify accurately in court about the particulars of a notarization without a journal to aid the Notary's memory.

- Journals of notarial acts prevent or abort baseless lawsuits by showing that a Notary did use reasonable care or that a transaction did occur as recorded. Journal thumbprints and signatures are especially effective in defeating such groundless suits.

- Requiring each document signer to leave a signature, or even a thumbprint, in the Notary's journal both deters attempted forgeries or other forms of fraud and provides strong evidence for a conviction should a fraud occur.

Journal Entries. The Notary's journal should contain the following information for each notarial act performed:

1) The date, time of day and type of notarization (jurat, acknowledgment, etc.)

2) The type (or title) of document notarized, including the number of pages and the date of the document

3) The signature, address and printed name of each document signer and witness

4) A statement as to how the signer was identified

- If by personal knowledge, the journal entry should read "Personal Knowledge."

- If by satisfactory evidence, the journal entry should contain either (a) a description of the ID card accepted, including the type of ID, the government agency issuing the ID, the ID's serial or identifying number and its date of issuance or expiration; or (b) the signature of any credible identifying witness and how that credible identifying witness was identified.

5) Any other pertinent information, including the fee charged for the notarial service or any peculiarities relating to the signer or the document

Journal Thumbprint. Increasingly, Notaries are asking document signers to leave a thumbprint in the journal. The journal thumbprint is a strong deterrent to forgery and other forms of fraud because it represents absolute proof of the criminal's identity and appearance. Nothing prevents a Notary from asking for a thumbprint for every notarial act, if the signer is willing. Refusal to leave a thumbprint is not, however, grounds for a Notary to deny a notarization.

Complete Entry Before Certificate. The Notary should complete the journal entry before filling out the notarial certificate on a document to prevent the signer from leaving with the notarized document before vital information is entered in the journal.

Never Surrender Journal. Notaries should never surrender control of their journals to anyone unless expressly subpoenaed by a court order. Even when an employer has paid for the Notary's official journal and seal, these items go with the Notary upon termination of employment. No one but the Notary may properly possess and use these tools of office.

Notarial Certificate

Requirement. In notarizing any document, a Notary must complete a notarial certificate. The certificate is wording that indicates exactly what the Notary has certified. The notarial certificate wording may appear on the document itself or on an attachment to it. The certificate should contain:

1) A venue indicating where the notarization is being performed: "State of New York, County of _____" is the typical venue wording, with the county name inserted in the blank. The letters "SS." or "SCT." sometimes appear after the venue; they abbreviate the traditional Latin word *scilicet*, meaning "in particular" or "namely."

2) A statement of particulars that indicates what the notarization has attested: An acknowledgment certificate might include such wording as: "On _____ (date) before

me, _____ (name of Notary), personally appeared _____ (name of signer), personally known to me (or proved to me on the basis of satisfactory evidence) to be the person(s)...." A jurat certificate might include such wording as: "Subscribed and sworn to (or affirmed) before me on _____ (date) by _____ (name of signer)."

3) A testimonium clause, which may be optional if the date is included in the statement of particulars: Typical wording for this clause is: "Witness my hand and official seal, this the _____ day of _____ (month), _____ (year)." In this short sentence, the Notary formally attests to the truthfulness of the preceding facts in the certificate. "Hand" means signature.

4) The official signature of the Notary, exactly as the name appears on the Notary's commission

5) The seal of the Notary, although not required by New York law: On many certificates the letters "L.S." appear, indicating where the seal is to be located. These letters abbreviate the Latin term *locus sigilli*, meaning "place of the seal." The impression made by an inking seal should be placed near but not over the letters so that wording imprinted by the seal will not be obscured. The impression made by an embossing seal, on the other hand, may be placed directly over the letters — slightly displacing portions of the characters and leaving a clue that document examiners can use to distinguish an original from a fraudulent photocopy.

6) Printed, typewritten or stamped information identifying the Notary: Since state law does not require Notaries to use a seal, a New York Notary is required to print, type or stamp, beneath his or her signature in black ink, the following information on every notarial certificate: the Notary's name, the words "Notary Public State of New York," the Notary's commission expiration date, the name of the county in which the Notary was originally qualified and, if applicable, the name of any county in which the Notary's certificate of official character has been filed, using the words "Certificate filed in _____ County." If the Notary has qualified or has filed a certificate of official character with the clerk in a county or counties within the city of New York, then

the Notary must also affix to each document in black ink the official number or numbers given to him or her by the clerk or clerks at the time the Notary qualified or filed the certificate. If the document is to be recorded in an office of the register of New York City in any county within the city and the Notary has been given a number or numbers by the register when the Notary registered his or her signature or certificate, then the Notary must affix this number or numbers to the document in black ink (Executive Law § 137).

Loose Certificates. When certificate wording is not preprinted on the document for the Notary to fill out, a loose certificate may be attached. Normally, this form is stapled to the document, either preceding or following the signature page. Only one side of the certificate should be stapled, so it can be lifted to show the document underneath.

To prevent a loose certificate from being removed and fraudulently placed on another document, there are precautions a Notary can take. The Notary can emboss the certificate and document together and then neatly print or type on the certificate, "Attached document bears embossment." The Notary also can print or type on the document that a loose certificate is attached and can print or type a brief description of the document on the certificate: "This certificate is attached to a _____ (title or type of document), dated _____, of _____ (number) pages, also signed by _____ (name[s] of other signer[s])."

While fraud-deterrent steps such as these can make it much more difficult for a loose certificate to be removed and misused, there is no absolute protection against its removal and misuse. Notaries must absolutely ensure that, while a certificate remains in their control, it is attached only to its intended document.

Do Not Pre-Sign/Seal Certificates. A Notary should never sign and/or seal certificates ahead of time or permit other persons to attach loose notarial certificates to documents. Nor should the Notary send an unattached, signed and sealed loose certificate through the mail, even if requested to do so by a signer who previously appeared before the Notary. These actions may facilitate fraud or forgery, and they could subject the Notary to lawsuits to recover damages resulting from the Notary's negligence or misconduct.

Selecting Certificates. It is not the role of the Notary to decide what type of certificate — and thus, what type of notarization — a document needs. As ministerial officials, Notaries generally follow instructions and fill out forms that have been provided for them. They do not issue instructions or decide which forms are appropriate in a given case. Selecting a notarial certificate in fact is considered the unauthorized practice of law and exposes the Notary to the attendant penalties. (See "Unauthorized Practice of Law," pages 60–61.)

If a document is presented to a Notary without certificate wording and if the signer doesn't know what type of notarization is appropriate, then the Notary should ask the signer to find out what kind of notarization and certificate are needed. Usually, the agency that issued the document or the one that will be receiving it can provide this information.

False Certificate. A Notary who completes a false notarial certificate with intent to defraud, deceive or injure another person may be guilty of forgery in the second degree, a Class D Felony punishable by a prison term of up to seven years, or of a Class E Felony, for which a prison term of up to four years may be imposed (Penal Law §§ 70.00, 170.10 and 175.40 and NPLL, "Definitions and General Terms: Acknowledgment"). An example of completing a false certificate would be if a Notary signed and sealed an acknowledgment certificate indicating that a signer personally appeared when the signer actually did not.

Notaries are often pressured by employers, clients, friends or relatives to be untruthful in their official certificates. An employer may ask the Notary to notarize a spouse's signature without the spouse's presence. A client may ask the Notary to take an acknowledgment over the phone. A friend or relative may ask the Notary to consider a stranger as personally known. In complying with these requests, the Notary would have to fill out a false certificate, which is a criminal act.

Certain Defects Do Not Invalidate Certificate. A Notary Public's certificate or act shall not be invalidated for any of the following reasons:

- The Notary was ineligible to be commissioned.

- The Notary's name was misspelled or some other error was made in the Notary's commission.

- The Notary failed to take or file the official oath of office or otherwise qualify for the commission.

- The Notary's commission was expired.

- The Notary vacated his or her commission by changing residence, accepting another public office or by any other action on the Notary's part.

- The Notary performed a notarization outside the jurisdiction where the Notary was authorized to act.

The Notary's certificate or act shall, on the other hand, be invalidated for any of the defects previously mentioned if, during the six months immediately after the act was performed, someone knew of the defect or the defect was apparent on the face of the Notary's certificate. After six months, however, the Notary's certificate or act will become valid (Executive Law § 142-a).

Notary Seal

Recommended. The National Notary Association recommends that Notaries affix an impression of an official seal on the certificate portion of every document notarized, although New York law does not require Notaries to do so.

Affixing a seal impression is a convenient way for the Notary to include required information on the certificate. (See "Required Information," page 56.) The seal also imparts an appropriate sense of ceremony to the notarial act.

Another practical reason for using a Notary seal is to prevent any rejection or delay of acceptance of notarized documents sent to other states and nations where the use of seals is a normal practice.

Embossing and Inking Seals. The seal may be either an inked stamp or an embosser. The inked stamp leaves a photographically reproducible impression, the embosser a raised impression.

In many states, county recording officials prefer inking seals because they considerably simplify the process of microfilming property deeds and other recordable documents. Recorders have to smudge seal embossments with carbon or other photocopiable substances before they can be microfilmed.

Format. The size and shape of the seal are left to the Notary. Most embossing seals are circular and most inking seals are rectangular.

Required Information. The New York Department of State advises that the Notary seal should identify the Notary and his or her authority and jurisdiction. The only wording that the Department requires on a seal therefore is the name of the Notary and the words "Notary Public State of New York" (NPLL, "Definitions and General Terms: Seal").

However, the seal may also conveniently include the information that the Notary must print, stamp or type in black ink beneath his or her signature on every notarial certificate (Executive Law § 137):

- The name of the Notary

- The words "Notary Public State of New York"

- The name of the county where the Notary originally qualified

- The Notary's commission expiration date

- Any additional required information, including but not limited to the following: (a) the name of the county in which the Notary's certificate of official character is filed, using the words "Certificate filed _____ County"; (b) if a Notary has qualified or filed a certificate of official character in a county within the city of New York, any official number given to him or her by that county; and (c) if a particular notarized document is to be recorded in any register's office in the city of New York, any official number that may have been given to the Notary by the register

While the omission of the above information may not invalidate the notarization of a particular document, it may subject the Notary to disciplinary action by the Secretary of State (Executive Law § 137).

Attorney at Law. A Notary who is an attorney licensed to practice law in New York may substitute the words "Attorney and Counselor at Law State of New York" for the words "Notary Public State of New York" (Executive Law § 137).

Placement of Seal Impression. The Notary's seal impression should be placed near the Notary's signature on the notarial certificate. Whenever possible — and especially with documents that will be submitted to a recording official — the Notary should avoid affixing the seal over any text on the document or certificate. Some recorders will reject documents if writing or document text intrudes within the borders of the Notary's seal. If there is no room for required stamp information, the Notary may have no choice but to complete and attach a loose certificate that duplicates the notarial wording on the document. With documents that will not be publicly recorded, however, the recipient may allow the Notary to affix the stamp or seal over boilerplate text — the standard preprinted clauses or sections — as long as the wording within the stamp or seal is not obscured.

L.S. The letters "L.S." — from the Latin *locus sigilli*, meaning "location of the seal" — appear on many notarial certificates to indicate where the Notary seal should be placed. Only an embossing seal may be placed over these letters. An inking seal should be placed near, but not over, the letters.

Fees for Notarial Services

Maximum Fees. The following maximum fees for performing notarial acts are allowed by New York law (NPLL, "Schedule of Fees"):

- Acknowledgments — $2. For taking an acknowledgment, the fee is not to exceed $2 for each acknowledger's signature, plus $2 for each witness sworn in. For example, for notarizing a single document with signatures of three persons appearing before the Notary, a maximum of $6 could be charged (Executive Law § 136).

- Oaths and Affirmations — $2. For administering an oath or affirmation, with or without a jurat certificate, the fee is not to exceed $2 per person, except where another fee is prescribed by statute (Executive Law § 136).

- Protests — 75¢. For executing a protest for nonpayment or nonacceptance, the maximum fee is 75¢. For each notice of protest, not exceeding five notices on any bill or note, the fee is 10¢ (Executive Law § 135).

- <u>Proofs of Execution by Subscribing Witness — $2</u>. For taking a proof of execution by a subscribing witness, the Notary may charge a maximum fee of $2 for each absent principal whose acknowledgment is proved by the subscribing witness , plus $2 for swearing in the subscribing witness (Executive Law § 136).

<u>Option Not to Charge</u>. Notaries are not required to charge for their services, and they may charge any fee less than the maximum.

<u>Overcharging</u>. Charging more than the legally prescribed fees may subject the Notary to removal from office, criminal prosecution and civil action in which the person overcharged may seek triple the damages from the Notary (Public Officers Law § 67).

<u>Seal Affixed Free of Charge</u>. A Notary may not charge any additional fee for affixing a seal on a certificate of protest or other notarial certificate (Executive Law § 135).

<u>No Fees Allowed for Certain Notaries</u>. No fee may be charged by a Notary who is on the staff of a county clerk and who has been designated by law to notarize for the public during normal business hours (Public Officers Law § 534).

<u>No Fees Allowed for Certain Oaths</u>. No fee may be charged by a Notary for administering the oath of office to a member of the legislature, to any military officer, to an inspector of elections or clerk of the poll or to any other public officer or public employee (Public Officers Law § 69).

<u>Dividing Fees with Attorney</u>. A New York Notary may not divide or agree to divide his or her fees with an attorney. In addition, the Notary may not accept any part of an attorney's fee for any legal business (NPLL, "Professional Conduct").

Disqualifying Interest

<u>Impartiality</u>. Notaries are appointed to be impartial, disinterested witnesses whose screening duties help ensure the integrity of important legal and commercial transactions. Lack of impartiality by a Notary throws doubt on the integrity and lawfulness of any transaction.

According to the New York Department of State, a Notary must not notarize if the Notary is a party to the document or if the Notary has a financial or beneficial interest in the document, and of course a Notary must never notarize his or her own signature (NPLL, "Appointment and Qualifications: Miscellaneous: Notary Public — Disqualifications").

Financial or Beneficial Interest. A financial or beneficial interest exists when the Notary is individually named as a principal in a financial transaction or when the Notary receives an advantage, right, privilege, property or fee valued at more than the lawfully prescribed notarial fee. For example, a Notary who is a grantee or mortgagee in a conveyance or mortgage is disqualified from taking the acknowledgment of the grantor or mortgagor, and of course a Notary who is the grantor may not take his or her own acknowledgment.

New York courts have voided documents notarized by persons who were financially and beneficially interested in the related transaction (NPLL, "Appointment and Qualifications: Miscellaneous: Notary Public — Disqualifications").

Corporations. A Notary who is a stockholder, director, officer or employee of a corporation may take an acknowledgment or proof of any person in the corporation who is executing a corporate instrument, may administer an oath or affirmation to any other stockholder, director, officer or employee of the corporation or protest for nonpayment any negotiable instrument owned or held for collection by the corporation. However, a Notary may not take an acknowledgment or proof if he or she is one of the parties executing the instrument or may financially benefit from the transaction (Executive Law § 138).

New York courts have held that an acknowledgment by one of the incorporators of other incorporators who signed a certificate was of no legal effect (NPLL, "Appointment and Qualifications: Miscellaneous: Notary Public — Disqualifications").

Attorney-Notaries. Notaries licensed to practice law in New York may, at their discretion, notarize for clients (Executive Law § 135).

Relatives. While notarizing for a family member is not directly prohibited in New York law or the NPLL, Notaries should not notarize for persons related by blood or marriage, because of the likelihood of a financial or beneficial interest.

A Notary will often have a clear-cut disqualifying financial or beneficial interest in notarizing for a close relative, especially a spouse. If the Notary's spouse, for example, purchases a home in which the couple will live, then the Notary should not notarize the spouse's signature on the deed.

It is often difficult for a Notary to retain impartiality with a close relative. Anyone, for example, is entitled to advise a relative to sign or not to sign an important document, but such action is entirely inappropriate for the impartial Notary.

Refusal of Services

Legal Requests for Services. Notaries must honor all lawful and reasonable requests to notarize (Penal Law § 195.00). It does not matter whether or not the person requesting the act is a client or customer of the Notary or the Notary's employer. In addition, a person's race, religion, nationality or political viewpoint is not due cause for refusing to perform a notarial act.

Noncustomer Discrimination Prohibited. A Notary employed by a private employer should not discriminate between customers and noncustomers. Fees and services provided should be the same for all individuals requesting a notarial act, whether or not the individual is a customer or client of the employer.

Penalty. Should a Notary knowingly, with intent to obtain a benefit or injure or deprive another person of a benefit, refuse to perform a notarial act when lawfully requested, the Notary may be subject to charges of official misconduct (Penal Law § 195.00).

Exception. A Notary may (and should) refuse to notarize a document if he or she knows that the document is blatantly fraudulent.

Unauthorized Practice of Law

Do Not Assist in Legal Matters. A nonattorney Notary may not give legal advice or accept fees for legal advice. As a ministerial official, the nonattorney Notary is not permitted to assist other persons in drafting, preparing, selecting, completing or understanding a document or transaction. The Notary should not fill in the blank spaces in the text of a document for other persons, tell others what documents they need or how to draft them or advise others about the legal sufficiency of a document

— and especially not for a fee. All these actions are considered to be the unauthorized practice of law.

In New York, the unauthorized practice of law is a misdemeanor. In addition, the state Supreme Court has the power to punish for criminal contempt any person who illegally practices law. As a result, the unauthorized practice of law by a Notary may cause the Notary to be removed from office by the Secretary of State, imprisoned and/or fined (Judiciary Law §§ 484, 485 and 750 and NPLL, "Restrictions and Violations: Illegal Practice of Law by Notary Public" and "Professional Conduct").

Of course, a Notary may fill in the blanks on the notarial certificate. And a Notary, as a private individual, may prepare legal documents that he or she is personally a party to. But the Notary then may not notarize his or her own signature on these documents.

<u>Do Not Determine Notarial Act.</u> A Notary who is not an attorney should not determine the type of notarial act to perform or decide which certificate to attach. This is beyond the scope of the Notary's expertise, is considered the unauthorized practice of law and exposes the Notary to all the potential penalties discussed above. The Notary should only follow instructions provided by the document, its signer, its issuing or receiving agency or an attorney.

If a document lacks notarial certificate wording, the Notary must ask the document signer what type of notarization is required. The Notary may then type the appropriate notarial wording on the document or attach a preprinted loose certificate. If the signer does not know what type of notarization is required, the issuing or receiving agency should be contacted. This decision is never to be made by the Notary unless the Notary is also an attorney.

<u>Exceptions.</u> Specially trained, nonattorney Notaries who are certified or licensed in a particular field (real estate, insurance, escrow, etc.) may offer advice or prepare documents related to that field only. Paralegals under the supervision of an attorney may give advice about documents in routine legal matters.

<u>Do Not Solicit for Attorney.</u> According to the New York Department of State, a Notary may not receive any compensation for referring a legal matter to a lawyer. A Notary is strictly prohibited from dividing fees with a lawyer or accepting any part of a lawyer's fee for any legal business (NPLL, "Professional Conduct").

Immigration Documents

Do Not Offer Advice. Nonattorney Notaries may never advise others on the subject of immigration or help others prepare immigration documents — and especially not for a fee. Under New York statute, Notaries who offer immigration advice to others may be prosecuted for the unauthorized practice of law (Judiciary Law §§ 484, 485 and 750 and NPLL, "Restrictions and Violations: Illegal Practice of Law by Notary Public" and "Professional Conduct"). (See "Unauthorized Practice of Law," pages 60–61.)

Immigration Assistance Service Provider. New York law now authorizes nonattorneys and entities to provide non-legal clerical and administrative immigration services under Article 28-C of the General Business Law. Persons and entities must be licensed, must obtain a $50,000–$250,000 bond (the amount is based upon total receipts for such services in a 12-month period) and must adhere to certain prescribed business practices and advertising restrictions. The provider may not include in any advertisement the claim that he or she is qualified to give legal advice on immigration matters or use the titles of "attorney" and "Notary Public" in order to convey the impression that the provider has special expertise in immigration matters. If the provider is in fact a Notary Public, however, then he or she may use the title "Notary Public" in advertising (General Business Law Article 28-C §§ 460-b and 460-e).

Common Documents. Affidavits are the forms issued or accepted by the U.S. Citizenship and Immigration Services (USCIS) that are most often notarized, with the Affidavit of Support (Form I-134) being the most common.

Non-USCIS-issued documents are often notarized and submitted in support of an immigration petition. These may include translator's declarations, statements from employers or banks and affidavits of relationship.

Naturalization Certificate Copies or Notarizations. The law imposes harsh penalties for printing or photocopying a certificate of naturalization without lawful authority. The National Notary Association recommends that a Notary only certify a copy of a certificate of naturalization if written directions are provided by a U.S. immigration authority.

Wills

Do Not Offer Advice. A Notary risks prosecution for the unauthorized practice of law if he or she advises a signer on how to proceed with a will (NPLL, "Professional Conduct"). (See "Unauthorized Practice of Law," pages 60–61.)

Executing Wills. The New York Department of State warns Notaries not to execute an acknowledgment certificate when asked to notarize a will: "Such acknowledgment cannot be deemed equivalent to an attestation clause accompanying a will" (NPLL, "Professional Conduct"). The attestation clause is the statement at the end of the will wherein the witnesses certify that the document was executed before them (NPLL, "Definitions and General Terms: Attestation Clause").

Furthermore, the NPLL cites *Matter of Flynn*, 142 Misc. 7, which strongly discourages the execution of wills under the supervision of a Notary who is in effect acting as an attorney (NPLL, "Restrictions and Violations: Wills").

Ill-informed advice may adversely affect the affairs of the signer. The format of a will is dictated by strict laws, and any deviation may result in nullification. In some cases, holographic (handwritten) wills have actually been voided by notarization.

Self-Proving Wills. New York law permits a will to be made "self-proving" at the request of the testator or after the testator's death. This is achieved through an affidavit, which states facts that, unless disproved, would establish the genuineness of the will, the validity of its execution and the testator's mental competency at the time of its execution. Attesting witnesses to the will must sign and swear to the truthfulness of the affidavit before a Notary or other officer authorized to administer oaths (Surrogate's Court Procedures Act § 1406).

Self-proving affidavits are designed to relieve the attesting witnesses of the need to appear in court when the will is probated.

Living Wills. Documents called living wills may be notarized. These are not actual wills but written statements of a signer's wishes concerning medical treatment in the event he or she is unable to issue instructions on his or her own behalf.

Advertising

False or Misleading Advertising. A Notary's commission may be subject to disciplinary action if the Notary advertises or claims to have powers not authorized by law. For example, a Notary may not claim to have authority to officially certify the translation of a document, since this is not a power given by New York law.

For practicing fraud or deceit in advertising, the Notary may be found guilty of a misdemeanor, his or her commission may be revoked or suspended by the Secretary of State and the Notary may be imprisoned, fined or both (Executive Law § 135-a and NPLL, "Professional Conduct" and "Restrictions and Violations: Executive Law").

Foreign-Language Advertising. A non-attorney Notary Public is prohibited from using any terms in a foreign-language advertisement that mean or imply that the Notary is an attorney licensed to practice law in New York or in any jurisdiction of the United States. An administrative rule effective December 11, 2012, specifies that a Notary Public, who is not an attorney licensed to practice law in the state of New York, may not falsely advertise by using foreign terms, including, but not limited to: abogado, mandataire, procuratore, Адвокат, 律師, and avoca (19 CRR-NY 200.1[a]).

In addition, a Notary must post the following statement in every foreign-language advertisement: "I am not an attorney licensed to practice law and may not give legal advice about immigration or any other legal matter or accept fees for legal advice." The statement must be written in the same language as the advertisement. "Advertisement" means material designed to give notice of or to promote the services offered by a Notary for profit and includes business cards, brochures and notices, whether in print or electronic form. An administrative rule provides disclaimers which must be posted in the same language as the advertisement in simplified Chinese, traditional Chinese, Spanish, Korean and Haitian Creole (19 CRR-NY 200.1[b]).

Any person who violates these foreign-language advertising provisions may be liable for a civil penalty of up to $1,000 recoverable in an action initiated by the Attorney General or at the request of the Secretary of State. In addition, the Secretary of State may suspend a Notary upon a second violation and upon a third violation, remove the Notary from office.

The new law requires the Secretary of State to designate by rule or regulation the terms in a foreign language that mean or imply that a Notary is licensed to practice law in New York and authorizes the Secretary to promulgate any other rules to implement the new law, including the statements that a Notary is required to post (Executive Law § 135-b, 19 CRR-NY 200.1).

False Documents

Notary Not Responsible. It is not the duty of the Notary to verify the truthfulness or accuracy of the facts in the text of a document. In fact, it would be a breach of the signer's privacy for Notaries to read the documents they notarize. The Notary is entitled, however, to quickly scan the document to extract important particulars (its title, date and number of pages, for example) to record in an official journal.

However, if a Notary happens to discover that a document is false or fraudulent, the Notary, as a responsible public official, has a duty to refuse the notarization and to report the attempted fraud to appropriate authorities. According to the New York Department of State, for administering an oath or affirmation on an affidavit that the Notary knows to be false, the Notary may be removed from office (NPLL, "Restrictions and Violations: Executive Law," and "Definitions and General Terms: Affidavit").

Blank or Incomplete Documents

Do Not Notarize. While New York law does not specifically address notarizing a blank or incomplete document, this is a dangerous, unbusinesslike practice and a breach of common sense, similar to signing a blank check.

A fraudulent document could readily be created above a Notary's signed and sealed certificate on an otherwise blank piece of paper. With documents containing blanks to be filled in after the notarization by a person other than the signer, there is a danger that the information inserted will be contrary to the wishes of the signer.

Any blanks in a document should be filled in by the signer. If the blanks are inapplicable and intended to be left unfilled, the signer should be asked to line through each space (using ink) or to write "Not Applicable" or "N/A."

Foreign Languages

Foreign-Language Documents. Any notarized document conveying title to real estate that is presented for recording in a county office must be completely in English, including the Notary's certificate and any authentication certificates. Proper names may be in a foreign language, as long as the letters used are English. A real-property conveyance written in a language other than English may only be recorded in New York if it is accompanied by a duly certified English-language translation (Real Property Law § 333).

New York Notaries are not prohibited from notarizing other types of documents written in a language other than English, provided that both the notarial certificate and document signature are in English or in a language that the Notary can read.

There are, however, difficulties to consider with foreign-language documents. Blatant fraud might be undetectable. The Notary seal might be misinterpreted in another country. Making a journal entry may be difficult.

If the Notary encounters difficulty with notarizing a foreign-language document, the signer could be referred to a Notary who can read the language. In large cities, such multilingual Notaries are often found in ethnic neighborhoods or foreign consulates.

Signers Who Speak a Foreign Language. There should always be direct communication between the Notary and document signer, whether in English or any other language. The Notary should never rely on an intermediary or interpreter to determine a signer's willingness or competence. A third party may have a motive for misrepresenting the circumstances to the Notary and/or to the signer.

Notarizing for Minors

Under Age 18. Generally, persons must reach the age of majority before they can handle their own legal affairs and sign documents for themselves. In New York, the age of majority is 18. Normally, natural guardians (parents) or court-appointed guardians will sign on a minor's behalf. In certain cases, where minors are engaged in business transactions or serving as court witnesses, they may lawfully sign documents and have their signatures notarized.

Include Age Next to Signature. When notarizing for a minor, the Notary should ask the signer to write his or her age next to the signature to alert any person relying on the document that the signer is a minor. The Notary is not required to verify the minor signer's age.

Identification. The method for identifying a minor is the same as that for an adult. However, determining the identity of a minor can be a problem because minors often do not possess acceptable identification documents such as driver's licenses or passports. If the minor does not have an acceptable ID document, then the other methods of identifying acknowledgers, either the Notary's personal knowledge of the minor or the oath of a credible identifying witness who can identify the minor, must be used.

Signature by Mark

Mark Serves as Signature. A person who cannot sign his or her name because of illiteracy or a physical disability may instead use a mark — an X, for example — as a signature, as long as there are two witnesses to the making of the mark.

Witnesses. For a signature by mark to be notarized, the National Notary Association recommends that there be two witnesses, in addition to the Notary, to the making of the mark.

The witnesses should sign the document and the Notary's journal. One witness should legibly print the marker's name in the journal and beside the mark on the document. It is recommended that a mark also be affixed in the Notary's journal.

Notarization Procedures. Because a properly witnessed mark is considered a signature under custom and law, no special notarial certificate is required. As with any other signer, the marker must be positively identified as required by New York law.

Electronic Signatures

Electronic Signatures Legal. In New York, an electronic signature may be used by a person in lieu of a handwritten signature. An electronic signature has the same validity and effect as a handwritten signature (State Technology Law § 104).

Exceptions. The sections of New York's State Technology Law (§§ 301-309) that govern electronic signatures do not apply to the following types of documents (State Technology Law § 307):

- A document providing for the disposition of an individual's person or property upon death or incompetence, or appointing a fiduciary of an individual's person or property, which includes wills, trusts, decisions consenting to orders not to resuscitate, powers of attorney and health care proxies, with the exception of contractual beneficiary designations

- Any negotiable instruments and other instruments of title in cases where possession of the document is deemed to confer title, unless an electronic version of the document is created, stored or transferred in a manner that allows for the existence of only one unique, identifiable and unalterable version which cannot be copied except in a form that is readily identifiable as a copy

- Any conveyance or other instrument recordable under Article Nine of the Real Property Law

- Any other document that the electronic facilitator charged with implementing the electronic signature provisions in the State Technology Law has specifically excepted

Electronic Recording. Effective September 23, 2012, a new law permits, but does not require, county recorders to accept electronic real property records signed with an electronic signature.

The new law states that any signature requirement for any document requiring acknowledgment or notarization as a condition for recording is satisfied by a "digitized wet signature" (signature of the Notary created by hand and scanned) and "digital stamp" (inked image of a physical Notary stamp impression scanned) of the individual, or an electronic signature. If the document is signed with an electronic signature, no physical or electronic image of a stamp, impression or seal is required to accompany the e-signature.

The bill also requires the state electronic facilitator to promulgate rules for electronic recording in general and for adequate information security protection to ensure that electronic real property records are accurate, authentic, adequately preserved for long-term electronic storage and resistant to tampering.

Electronic Signatures Defined. An administrative rule, which became effective December 11, 2012, specified that electronic signatures used by a Notary on an instrument affecting real property shall be:

- Unique to the Notary

- Capable of independent verification

- Under the Notary's sole control

- Attached to, or logically associated with, the electronic record in such a manner that it can be determined if any data contained in the electronic record has been changed subsequent to the electronic notarization (9 CRR-NY 540.7[e])

Notarization Procedures Established. Notaries who perform a notarization of an instrument affecting real property that exists as an electronic record must do so only when the signer appears before the Notary in person at the time of the notarization. In addition, Notaries must identify the signer as prescribed by New York state law (19 CRR-NY 540.7[e]). (See "Identifying Document Signers", pages 45–46.)

Military-Officer Notarizations

May Notarize Worldwide. Certain U.S. military personnel may notarize anywhere in the world for other military personnel and certain associated groups, as stipulated by the U.S. Code, Title 10, Subtitle A, Part II, Chapter 53 § 1044a(b). Based on that code, the following persons are authorized to act as Notaries:

- Judge advocates, including reserve judge advocates when not in a duty status

- Civilian attorneys serving as legal assistance attorneys

- Adjutants, assistant adjutants and personnel adjutants, including reserve members when not in a duty status

- Other members of the armed forces, including reserve members when not in a duty status, so authorized by armed-forces regulations or by statute

Validity of Notarial Acts. The signature of any of the above when acting as a Notary, together with the title of that individual's office, is considered proof that the signature is genuine, that the individual holds the designated title and that he or she is authorized to perform notarial acts (USC Title 10 § 1044a[d]).

Fees. Military-officer Notaries may not charge or receive a fee for performing a notarial act (USC Title 10 § 1044a[c]).

Real-Property Acknowledgments. New York law stipulates that acknowledgments affecting the transfer of real property located within the state of New York may be taken only by a commissioned officer in active service with the rank of second lieutenant or higher (in the Army, Air Force or Marine Corps) or ensign or higher (in the Navy or Coast Guard) or with the equivalent rank in any other part of the U.S. armed forces.

The notarial certificate for such acknowledgments must state the rank and serial number of the officer who performed the notarization, as well as the command to which he or she is attached. The certificate also must include the serial number of the person who makes the acknowledgment, or whose dependent does so, if that person is enlisted or commissioned in the U.S. armed forces. The venue of such acknowledgments need not be disclosed.

For this specific type of notarization, New York law stipulates that no authentication of the officer's signature is necessary (Real Property Law § 300).

Reasonable Care

Responsibility. As public servants, Notaries must act responsibly and exercise reasonable care in the performance of their official duties. If a Notary fails to do so, he or she may be subject to a civil lawsuit to recover financial damages caused by the Notary's error or omission.

In general, reasonable care is that degree of concern and attentiveness that a person of normal intelligence and responsibility would exhibit. If a Notary can show to a judge or jury that he or she did everything expected of a reasonable person, then the judge or jury is obligated by law to find the Notary blameless and not liable for damages.

Complying with all pertinent laws is the first rule of reasonable care for a Notary. If there are no statutory guidelines in a given instance, then the Notary should go to extremes to use common sense and prudence. (See "Steps to Proper Notarization," pages 15–20.)

Journal. Although a journal is not required by New York law, a Notary's best proof of having exercised reasonable care is a detailed, accurate journal of notarial acts. Such entries as the serial numbers of identification documents and the signatures of credible identifying witnesses can show that the Notary took appropriate steps to positively identify every signer. Possession by the Notary of a well-maintained journal can prevent lawsuits that falsely claim that the Notary was negligent.

Authentication

Documents Sent Out of State. Documents notarized in New York and sent to other states and nations may be required to bear proof that the Notary's signature and seal are genuine and that the Notary had the authority to act at the time of notarization. This process of proving the genuineness of an official signature and seal is called authentication or legalization. The proof usually is in the form of a certificate, which may be known by different names: certificates of authority, certificates of capacity, certificates of authenticity, certificates of prothonotary and "flags."

In New York, the proof is called an authentication certificate and is attached to the notarized document by the county clerk's office where the Notary's commission or certificate of official character is filed (Executive Law §§ 132 and 133 and NPLL, "Introduction").

The county clerk may charge a $3 fee for issuing an authentication certificate for attachment to a notarized document. The county clerk in the county in which a New York Notary's commission is filed already has a copy of the Notary's official signature and may issue an authentication certificate without further action on the part of the Notary. A New York Notary who expects to notarize regularly in one or more other counties may file a signature sample and certificate of official character in any such additional counties, thus permitting these counties to issue authentication certificates for that Notary. A county clerk will charge the Notary $10 for filing a certificate of official character (Executive Law §§ 132 and 133 and NPLL, "Introduction").

For a notarized document being sent from New York to another U.S. state or territory, a certificate from the county clerk is normally sufficient authentication. However, if an authentication certificate from the New York Department of State is necessary in addition to the county clerk's authentication certificate, the New York Department of State may charge $10 (DOS website, "Apostille").

The New York Department of State issues authentication certificates at two locations:

Department of State	Department of State
State Records Bureau	Certification Unit
One Commerce Plaza	123 William Street, 19th Floor
99 Washington Avenue	New York, NY 10038-3804
Albany, NY 12231-0001	(212) 417-5747
(518) 473-1001	

Documents Sent Out of Country. If the notarized document is going out of the United States, a chain authentication process may be necessary. Additional certificates of authority may have to be obtained from the U.S. Department of State in Washington, DC, a foreign consulate in Washington, DC, and a ministry of foreign affairs in the particular foreign nation.

Apostilles and the Hague Convention. More than 100 nations, including the United States, subscribe to a treaty under the Hague Convention that simplifies authentication of notarized documents exchanged between any of these nations. The official name of this treaty, adopted by the Convention on October 5, 1961, is *The Hague Convention Abolishing the Requirement of Legalization for Foreign Public Documents*. (For a list of the subscribing countries, see "Hague Convention Nations," pages 127–129.)

Under the Hague Convention, only one authentication certificate, called an *apostille*, is necessary to ensure acceptance in these subscribing countries. (*Apostille* is French for "notation.")

In New York, *apostilles* are issued by the Department of State's office for $10 per certificate. Unfortunately, New York also requires the notarized document to bear an authentication certificate from the county clerk before issuing an *apostille* (DOS website, "Apostille"). In most other states, the *apostille* is the only authenticating form required.

A request for an *apostille* must be made in writing and must include the name, address and telephone number of the person making the request. The letter must also identify the nation to which the document will be sent. The person requesting the *apostille* should send the letter, the notarized document(s) bearing the county's authentication certificate and the $10 fee for each *apostille* (payable to "New York Department of State") to one of the Department of State offices listed above (DOS website, "Apostille").

It is not the Notary's responsibility to obtain an *apostille*. It is the responsibility of the party sending the document abroad.

MISCONDUCT, FINES AND PENALTIES

Misconduct

Misconduct Defined. In New York, a Notary is guilty of official misconduct when, with intent to obtain a benefit or to injure or deprive another person of a benefit, the Notary does either of the following (Penal Law § 195.00):

1) Knowingly performs an unauthorized notarial act or other act related to the function of the Notary

2) Knowingly and without due cause refuses to perform an authorized notarial act

Penalty for Misconduct. For any act of official misconduct by a Notary, the New York Secretary of State may suspend the commission of the Notary, meaning the Notary is prohibited from practicing for a specific period of time. The Secretary of State also has the option of removing the Notary from office or imposing a fine. None of these three penalties may be imposed, however, without first giving the accused Notary the chance to respond to the charges (Executive Law § 130).

In addition, criminal and civil suits against the Notary may result from an act of misconduct, and a Notary is liable for any and all damages to parties injured (Executive Law § 135). Official misconduct by a Notary is a Class A Misdemeanor, which is punishable by a prison term of up to one year or a fine of up to $1,000 (Penal Law §§ 70.15, 80.05 and 195.00).

Falsely Acting as a Notary. Any person who is not a Notary and who represents him- or herself as a Notary Public is guilty of a misdemeanor (Executive Law § 135-a).

In addition, a Notary who performs notarial acts before taking the oath of office is guilty of a misdemeanor (Public Officers Law § 15 and NPLL, "Restrictions and Violations: Public Officers Law").

Dishonesty or Fraud. Commission of an act involving dishonesty, fraud or deceit with the intent to substantially benefit the Notary or another, or to substantially injure another, is included in the definition of official misconduct. Such misconduct is a Class A Misdemeanor, punishable by a prison term of up to one year or a fine of up to $1,000 (Penal Law §§ 70.15, 80.05 and 195.00 and Executive Law § 135-a).

Application Misstatement. Substantial and material misstatement or omission in the application for a Notary commission is reason for the Secretary of State to revoke, suspend or refuse to grant a Notary's commission (NPLL, "Restrictions and Violations: Executive Law").

Felony Conviction. Conviction of a felony or of any offense involving moral depravity — such as engaging in prostitution or vagrancy, or possessing or distributing drugs — or of a nature incompatible with notarial duties, such as forgery, is reason for the Secretary of State to revoke, suspend or refuse to grant a Notary's commission (Executive Law § 130).

Telephone Notarizations. The practice of taking acknowledgments and affidavits over the telephone without the personal appearance of the signer is illegal (NPLL, "Professional Conduct").

The NPLL specifies that taking an acknowledgment over the telephone is a misdemeanor. Citing *Matter of Brooklyn Bar Assoc.*, 225 App. Div. 680, the NPLL state that, unless the person making the acknowledgment actually and personally appears before the Notary on the date specified, the Notary's certification that the person did so is palpably false and fraudulent (NPLL, "Definitions and General Terms: Acknowledgment.")

Citing *Matter of Napolis*, 169 App. Div. 469, the NPLL states that a Notary cannot administer an oath or affirmation over the telephone. Again, the oath-taker or affirmant must personally appear before the Notary at the time that he or she takes the oath or affirmation (NPLL, "Definitions and General Terms: Oath").

Failure to Affix Required Information. A Notary must print, type or stamp, beneath his or her signature in black ink, the following information on each instrument: the Notary's name, the words "Notary Public State of New York," the name of the county in which the Notary originally qualified, the Notary's commission expiration date and the name of any county in which the Notary has filed a certificate of official character, stated as "Certificate filed in _____ County." Failure to include such information may subject the Notary to disciplinary action by the Secretary of State (Executive Law § 137).

Refusal of Services. Notaries must honor all lawful and

reasonable requests to notarize. Should a Notary refuse to perform a lawful notarial act with the intent to obtain a benefit or to injure or deprive another person of a benefit, he or she may be subject to charges of official misconduct. This is a Class A Misdemeanor, for which a prison term of up to one year or a fine of up to $1,000 may be imposed (Penal Law §§ 70.15, 80.05 and 195.00).

Overcharging. A Notary who charges more than the legally prescribed fees is subject to removal from office and criminal or civil penalties, including criminal prosecution and civil action in which the person overcharged may seek triple the damages (Public Officers Law § 67).

Unauthorized Practice of Law. The unauthorized practice of law by a Notary who is not a lawyer is reason for removal from office by the Secretary of State. In addition, the person faces imprisonment, a fine or both (NPLL, "Professional Conduct").

A Notary may not give advice on the law, ask for and receive legal business for money or other consideration, send business to a lawyer, divide or agree to divide notarial fees with a lawyer, accept any portion of a lawyer's fee for any legal business or advertise that the Notary has powers not duly granted. A Notary also cannot counsel, advise or assist other persons in drafting, preparing, completing or understanding a document or transaction (Judiciary Law § 484 and NPLL, "Restrictions and Violations: Illegal Practice of Law by Notary Public" and "Professional Conduct").

In addition to being subject to penalties imposed by the Secretary of State, a Notary Public who engages in the unauthorized practice of law may be guilty of a misdemeanor (Judiciary Law § 485). The Supreme Court also has the power to prosecute for criminal contempt any person who unlawfully practices or assumes to practice law (Judiciary Law § 750).

Immigration Advice. Even if a Notary is licensed and bonded as an immigration assistance service provider, the Notary may not provide legal advice on immigration matters. (See "Immigration Documents," page 62.) Under New York statute, a nonattorney Notary who offers immigration advice to others may be prosecuted for the unauthorized practice of law (Judiciary Law §§ 484, 485 and 750 and NPLL, "Restrictions and Violations: Illegal Practice of Law by Notary Public" and "Professional Conduct"). (See "Unauthorized Practice of Law," pages 60–61.)

Naturalization Certificate Copies or Notarizations. A Notary may be in violation of federal law if he or she makes a typewritten, photostatic or any other copy of a certificate of naturalization or notarizes such a copy.

False or Misleading Advertising. The use of false or misleading advertising by a Notary to represent that he or she has duties, rights and privileges not given by law is reason for the Secretary of State to remove the Notary from office and subjects the Notary to possible imprisonment, fines or both (Executive Law § 135-a and NPLL, "Professional Conduct" and "Restrictions and Violations: Executive Law").

False Statements. A person is guilty of perjury if he or she has stated, under oath or affirmation, that a statement was true when he or she knew the statement was false (NPLL, "Restrictions and Violations: Perjury").

The Notary will be subject to removal from office for administering an oath or affirmation in reference to a statement the Notary knows to be false (NPLL, "Restrictions and Violations: Executive Law" and "Definitions and General Terms: Affidavit").

False Certificates. A Notary who knowingly completes a false notarial certificate may be guilty of forgery in the second degree, a Class D Felony punishable by a prison term of up to seven years, or of a Class E Felony, for which a prison term of up to four years may be imposed. Both Class D and Class E Felonies also are punishable by a fine not exceeding the higher of $5,000 or double the amount of the defendant's gain from the commission of the crime. In addition, any injured party may recover damages against a Notary who issues a false certificate (Penal Law §§ 70.00, 80.00, 170.10 and 175.40 and NPLL, "Definitions and General Terms: Acknowledgment").

False Acknowledgment. A Notary may not take an acknowledgment unless the Notary has personal knowledge or satisfactory evidence that the person making the acknowledgment is the same person that is described in the document (Real Property Law § 303).

A Notary who executes a fraudulent acknowledgment or proof of a conveyance of real property will be held liable for damages to any person injured (Real Property Law § 330). If, for example, a lender accepts a forged, notarized deed as collateral for a loan, the lender might sue the Notary who witnessed the bogus deed to recover losses.

Failure to Administer Oath or Affirmation. Notaries must administer oaths and affirmations in specific forms and as required by law. If a Notary refuses to perform a duty imposed by law, he or she may be charged with a Class A Misdemeanor, for which a prison term of up to one year or a fine of up to $1,000 may be imposed (Penal Law §§ 70.15 80.05 and 195.00 and NPLL, "Restrictions and Violations: Notary Must Officiate on Request").

Civil Lawsuit

Liability for Damages. For any misconduct by a Notary in performing official duties, the Notary is liable for all damages to any person injured (Executive Law § 135).

Right to Respond to Charges

Revocation or Suspension. Before the Secretary of State can suspend or revoke a commission due to professional misconduct, the accused Notary will have the chance to respond to the charges in a hearing (Executive Law § 130). ■

Test Your Knowledge

Trial Exam

Instructions. This exam is designed to test your knowledge of the basic concepts of notarization. It will also help you prepare for the proctored New York Notary Public exam that you must pass before being commissioned as a New York Notary. The questions here, of course, are not the same as those on the official test. Also, the Notary Public exam is made up of multiple-choice questions, with no true/false, fill-in-the-blank or essay questions as in this trial exam.

Work through this exam without looking at the answers, then check your responses and note where you need additional study. The answers can be found by carefully reviewing "Notary Laws Explained" (pages 21–77), the reprinted Notary statutes (pages 85–117), "10 Most-Asked Questions" (pages 10–14) and "Steps to Proper Notarization" (pages 15–20).

Scoring. A perfect score on this exam is 100 points. There are:

- 20 true/false questions worth 1 point each.
- 5 multiple-choice questions worth 4 points each.
- 5 fill-in-the-blank questions worth 4 points each.
- 5 essay questions worth 8 points each.

Now, get a separate sheet of paper and a pen or pencil, and get ready to test your knowledge.

True/False. For the following statements, answer true or false. Each correct answer is worth 1 point:

1) Notaries may act only in the county where they are commissioned. True or false?

2) The maximum Notary fee for taking the acknowledgment of two signers is $2. True or false?

3) Oaths and affirmations have the same legal effect. True or false?

4) Protests are one of the most common forms of notarization. True or false?

5) Notaries are obligated to ensure the truthfulness of the statements in the documents they notarize. True or false?

6) It is the duty of the Notary to decide what type of notarization is appropriate for a given document. True or false?

7) Though not legally required in New York, the use of a Notary seal and journal is a good practice. True or false?

8) In addition to the principal signer, a subscribing witness must sign the document. True or false?

9) An employee of a corporation may notarize for the officers and stockholders of that corporation. True or false?

10) Notaries may use their own wills as models in advising clients about how to handle their estates. True or false?

11) An oath for a deposition may be given over the telephone. True or false?

12) An acknowledged document, such as a deed, must be signed in the Notary's presence. True or false?

13) A Social Security card and a birth certificate offer reliable proof of a document signer's identity. True or false?

14) An affiant must do more than merely nod in assent to an oath. True or false?

15) The letters "SS." indicate that Notaries must write in their Social Security numbers. True or false?

16) Certifying a copy is not an official notarial act in New York. True or false?

17) It is a bad idea to notarize a document whose blank spaces will be filled in later. True or false?

18) On a notarial certificate, the venue indicates where the Notary's oath has been filed. True or false?

19) Although technically different, the terms "affiant" and "deponent" are sometimes interchanged. True or false?

20) Notaries may not perform acknowledgments on Sunday. True or false?

Multiple Choice. Choose the one best answer to each question. Each correct answer is worth 4 points.

1) In executing an acknowledgment, a Notary certifies that ...
   a. The signer took an oath or affirmation.
   b. The signer was positively identified by the Notary.
   c. The signer signed in the Notary's presence.

2) In executing a jurat, a Notary certifies that ...
   a. The signer was positively identified by the Notary.
   b. The signer was given an oath or affirmation by the Notary.
   c. The signer has no direct interest in the document.

3) Non-English-language real-property conveyances ...
   a. Cannot be notarized in New York.
   b. Are illegal in New York.
   c. Cannot be recorded in New York without a translation.

4) Notaries may be liable ...
   a. Only for their intentional acts of misconduct.
   b. Only for damages suffered by the signer.
   c. For all damages caused by their misconduct.

5) It could be the unauthorized practice of law to ...
   a. Explain a paragraph in an immigration document.
   b. Provide a notarial certificate requested by the signer.
   c. Type a paper following the signer's instructions.

Fill in the Blank. Write in the word or phrase that best completes each sentence. Each correct answer is worth 4 points.

1) A(n) _____ often must be attached to a notarized document sent out of state.

2) An affirmation is a solemn, spoken pledge that does not refer to a(n) _____.

3) The best ID cards contain the following three elements: _____; _____; and _____.

4) Without ID cards or personal knowledge of a signer's identity, Notaries may rely on the oath of a(n) _____ to identify a stranger.

5) The state official who appoints and regulates New York Notaries is the _____.

Essay. Reply to each question or statement with a short paragraph. Each complete and correct response is worth 8 points.

1) Under what conditions should a Notary execute a protest?

2) Why do most Notaries never execute depositions?

3) Why is a Social Security card all but worthless as an ID?

4) Why is it unwise for Notaries to notarize for relatives?

5) What are the differences between an acknowledgment certificate and a jurat?

Test Answers

True/False. 1. F; 2. F; 3. T; 4. F; 5. F; 6. F; 7. T; 8. T; 9. T; 10. F; 11. F; 12. F; 13. F; 14. T; 15. F; 16. T; 17. T; 18. F; 19. T; 20. F

<u>Multiple Choice</u>. 1. b; 2. b; 3. c; 4. c; 5. a

<u>Fill In the Blank</u>. 1. certificate of authentication; 2. Supreme Being; 3. photograph, signature and physical description; 4. credible identifying witness; 5. Secretary of State

<u>Essay</u>. Responses should include the basic information in the paragraphs below:

1) Since protests are complicated notarial acts, Notaries should only execute them if they understand the legal and financial terminology used in the protest certificate, or if they are under the supervision of a person with such an understanding.

2) Depositions are normally executed by professional shorthand reporters who are able to readily transcribe oral testimony. Also, because strict rules of procedure dictate how depositions are executed, Notaries without appropriate training or supervision should not attempt them.

3) A Social Security card is very easily counterfeited and has only one of the three vital elements of a good ID: a signature. Reliable IDs also bear a photograph and a physical description.

4) Although New York law does not specifically prohibit notarizing for family members, in doing so a Notary may violate restrictions against notarizing with a financial interest, especially in the case of spouses, parents and children. Notaries should fully live up to their roles as impartial witnesses and never notarize for close relatives.

5) An acknowledgment certificate certifies that the signer of the document personally appeared before the Notary on the date and in the county indicated, that the signer's identity was satisfactorily proven to the Notary and that the signer acknowledged having signed freely. A jurat certifies that the signer personally appeared before the Notary on the date and in the county indicated, that an oath or affirmation was administered to the signer by the Notary and that the document was signed in the Notary's presence.

Tally Your Score

After checking your answers, add up your score. Then look at the grading scale below to determine how you stand:

- 90–100: Excellent!
- 80–89: Good, but some review needed.
- 70–79: Fair. Reread the parts of the *Primer* covering the answers you missed.
- Below 70: Below par. Study the laws again thoroughly. ■

New York Laws Pertaining to Notaries Public

Reprinted on the following pages are pertinent sections of the New York *Notary Public License Law*, distributed to newly commissioned Notaries by the New York Department of State.

This official information contains sections of New York statutes that affect Notaries and notarial acts, mostly drawn from the Executive Law, Judiciary Law, Penal Law, Public Officers Law and Real Property Law.

It also contains helpful instructions on notarial matters not contained in the statutes.

NEW YORK STATE
NOTARY PUBLIC LICENSE LAW

Department of State
Division of Licensing Services

INTRODUCTION

Notary publics [sic] are commissioned by the Secretary of State. An applicant for a notary public commission must submit to the Division of Licensing Services an original application and $60 fee. The application includes an oath of office, which must be sworn and notarized. In addition to the application form and fee, the applicant must submit a "pass slip" showing that s/he has taken and passed the notary public examination. Examinations are regularly scheduled throughout the state. An individual admitted to practice in NYS as an attorney, may be appointed a notary public without an examination. The term of commission is 4 years.

Notary publics [sic] are commissioned in their counties of residence. After receiving and approving an applicant for a notary public commission, the Secretary of State forwards the commission, the original oath of office and the signature of the notary public to the appropriate county clerk. The county clerk maintains a record of the commission and signature. The public may then access this record and verify the "official" signature of the notary at the county clerk's office.

Upon request, county clerks will authenticate the signature of the notary on a document and will attest to the notary's authority to sign. This is normally obtained when the documents will be used outside the State. Notaries who expect to sign documents regularly in counties other than that of their residence may elect to file a certificate of official character with other New York State county clerks.

Out-of-State Residents. Attorneys, residing out of State, who are admitted to practice in the State and who maintain a law office within the State are deemed to be residents of the county where the office is maintained. Nonresidents other than attorneys who have offices or places of business in New York State may also become notaries. The oath of office and signature of the notary must be filed in the office of the county clerk of the county in which the office or place of business is located.

PROFESSIONAL CONDUCT

Use of the office of notary in other than the specific, step-by-step procedure required is viewed as a serious offense by the Secretary of State. The practice of taking acknowledgments and affidavits over the telephone, or otherwise, without the actual, personal appearance of the individual making the acknowledgment or affidavit before the officiating notary, is illegal.

The attention of all notaries public is called to the following judicial declarations concerning such misconduct:

"The court again wishes to express its condemnation of the acts of notaries taking acknowledgments or affidavits without the presence of the party whose acknowledgment is taken for the affiant, and that it will treat serious professional misconduct the act of any notary thus violating his official duty." (*Matter of Napolis*, 169 App. Div. 469, 472.)

"Upon the faith of these acknowledgments rests the title of real property, and the only security to such titles is the fidelity with which notaries and commissioners of deeds perform their duty in requiring the appearance of parties to such instruments before them and always refusing to execute a certificate unless the parties are actually known to them or the identity of the parties executing the instruments is satisfactorily proved." (*Matter of Gottheim*, 153 App. Div. 779, 782.)

Equally unacceptable to the Secretary of State is slipshod administration of oaths. **The simplest form in which an oath may be lawfully administered is:**

"Do you solemnly swear that the contents of this affidavit subscribed by you is [sic] correct and true?" (*Bookman v. City of New York*, 200 N.Y. 53, 56.)

Alternatively, the following affirmation may be used for persons who conscientiously decline taking an oath. This affirmation is legally equivalent to an oath and is just as binding:

"Do you solemnly, sincerely and truly declare and affirm that the statements made by you are true and correct?"

Whatever the form adopted, it must be in the presence of an officer authorized to administer it, and it must be an unequivocal and present act by which the affiant consciously takes upon himself the obligation of an oath. (Idem, citing People ex rel. *Kenyon v. Sutherland*, 81 N.Y. 1; *O'Reilly v. People*, 86 N.Y. 154, 158, 161.)

Unless a lawyer, the notary public may not engage directly or indirectly in the practice of law. Listed below are some of the activities involving the practice of law which are prohibited, and which subject the notary public to removal from office by the Secretary of State, and possible imprisonment, fine or both. A notary:

1. **May not give advice on the law.** The notary may not draw any kind of legal papers, such as wills, deeds, bills of sale, mortgages, chattel mortgages, contracts, leases, offers, options, incorporation papers, releases, mechanics liens, power of attorney, complaints and all legal pleadings, papers in summary proceedings to evict a tenant, or in bankruptcy, affidavits, or any papers which our courts have said are legal documents or papers.

2. **May not ask for and get legal business** to send to a lawyer or lawyers with whom he has any business connection or from whom he receives any money or other consideration for sending the business.

3. **May not divide or agree to divide his fees** with a lawyer, or accept any part of a lawyer's fee on any legal business.

4. **May not advertise in, or circulate** in any manner, any paper or advertisement, or say to anyone that he has any powers or rights not given to the notary by the laws under which the notary was appointed.

A notary public is cautioned not to execute an acknowledgment of the execution of a will. Such acknowledgment cannot be deemed equivalent to an attestation clause accompanying a will. (*See definition of Attestation Clause.*)

APPOINTMENT AND QUALIFICATIONS

Index

Law	Sec	Subject
Executive Law	133	Certification of Notarial Signatures
Executive Law	140	Commissioner of Deeds, NYC
Election Law	3-200 & 3-400	Commissioner of Elections
Public Officers Law	3	Qualifications for Holding Office
County Law	534	County Clerk; Appointment of Notaries
NYS Constitution	Art. III Sec. 7	Member of Legislature
NYS Constitution	Art. XIII Sec. 13-a	Sheriffs
Miscellaneous		Disqualifications

Executive Law
§130. Appointment of notaries public.

The Secretary of State may appoint and commission as many notaries public for the State of New York as in his or her judgment may be deemed best, whose jurisdiction shall be co-extensive with the boundaries of the state. The appointment of a notary public shall be for a term of 4 years. An application for an appointment as notary public shall be in form and set forth such matters as the Secretary of State shall prescribe. Every person appointed as notary public must, at the time of his or her appointment, be a citizen of the United States and either a resident of the State of New York or have an office or place of business in New York State. A notary public who is a resident of the State and who moves out of the state but still maintains a place of business or an office in New York State does not vacate his or her office as a notary public. A notary public who is a nonresident and who ceases to have an office or place of business in this state, vacates his or her office as a notary public. A notary public who is a resident of New York State and moves out of the state and who does not retain an office or place of business in this State shall vacate his or her office as a notary public. A non-resident who accepts the office of notary public in this State thereby appoints the Secretary of State as the person upon whom process can be served on his or her behalf. Before issuing to any applicant a commission as notary public, unless he or she be an attorney and counselor at law duly admitted to practice in this state or a court clerk of the Unified Court System who has been appointed to such position after taking a Civil Service promotional examination in the court clerk series of titles, the Secretary of State shall satisfy himself or herself that the applicant is of good moral character, has the equivalent of a common school education and is familiar with the duties and responsibilities of a notary public; provided, however, that where a notary public applies, before the expiration of his or her term, for reappointment with the county clerk or where a person whose term as notary public shall have expired applies within 6 months thereafter for reappointment as a notary public with the county clerk, such qualifying requirements may be waived by the Secretary of State, and further, where an application for reappointment is filed with the county clerk after the expiration of the aforementioned renewal period by a person who failed or was unable to re-apply by reason of his or her induction or enlistment in the armed forces of the United States, such qualifying requirements may also be waived by the Secretary of State, provided such application for reappointment is made within a period of 1 year after the military discharge of the applicant under conditions other than dishonorable. In any case, the appointment or reappointment of any applicant is in the discretion of the Secretary of State. The Secretary of State may suspend or remove from office, for misconduct, any notary public appointed by him or her but no such removal shall be made unless the person who is sought to be removed shall have been served with a copy of the charges against him or her and have an opportunity of being heard. No person shall be appointed as a notary public under this article who has been convicted, in this State or any other state or territory, of a felony or any of the following offenses, to wit:

(a) illegally using, carrying or possessing a pistol or other dangerous weapon;

(b) making or possessing burglar's instruments;

(c) buying or receiving or criminally possessing stolen property;

(d) unlawful entry of a building;

(e) aiding escape from prison;

(f) unlawfully possessing or distributing habit forming narcotic drugs;

(g) violating §§270, 270-a, 270-b, 270-c, 271, 275, 276, 550, 551, 551-a and subdivisions 6, 8, 10 or 11 of §722 of the former Penal Law as in force and effect immediately prior to September 1, 1967, or violating §§165.25, 165.30, subdivision 1 of §240.30, subdivision 3 of §240.35 of the Penal Law, or violating §§478, 479, 480, 481, 484, 489 and 491 of the Judiciary Law; or

(h) vagrancy or prostitution, and who has not subsequent to such conviction received an executive pardon therefor or a certificate of good conduct from the parole board to remove the disability under this section because of such conviction. A person regularly admitted to practice as an attorney and counselor in the courts of record of this state, whose office for the practice of law is within the State, may be appointed a notary public and retain his office as such notary public although he resides in or removes to an adjoining state. For the purpose of this and the following sections of this article such person shall be deemed a resident of the county where he maintains such office.

§131. Procedure of appointment; fees and commissions.

1. Applicants for a notary public commission shall submit to the Secretary of State with their application the oath of office, duly executed before any person authorized to administer an oath, together with their signature.

2. Upon being satisfied of the competency and good character of applicants for appointment as notaries public, the Secretary of State shall issue a commission to such persons; and the official signature of the applicants and the oath of office filed with such applications shall take effect.

3. The Secretary of State shall receive a non-refundable application fee of $60 from applicants for appointment, which fee shall be submitted together with the application. No further fee shall be paid for the issuance of the commission.

4. A notary public identification card indicating the appointee's name, address, county and commission term shall be transmitted to the appointee.

5. The commission, duly dated, and a certified copy or the original of the oath of office and the official signature, and $20 apportioned from the application fee shall be transmitted by the Secretary of State to the county clerk in which the appointee resides by the 10th day of the following month.

6. The county clerk shall make a proper index of commissions and official signatures transmitted to that office by the Secretary of State pursuant to the provisions of this section.

7. Applicants for reappointment of a notary public commission shall submit to the county clerk with their application the oath of office, duly executed before any person authorized to administer an oath, together with their signature.

8. Upon being satisfied of the completeness of the application for reappointment, the county clerk shall issue a commission to such persons; and the official signature of the applicants and the oath of office filed with such applications shall take effect.

9. The county clerk shall receive a non-refundable application fee of $60 from each applicant for reappointment, which fee shall be submitted together with the application. No further fee shall be paid for the issuance of the commission.

10. The commission, duly dated, and a certified or original copy of the application, and $40 apportioned from the application fee plus interest as may be required by statute shall be transmitted by the county clerk to the Secretary of State by the 10th day of the following month.

11. The Secretary of State shall make a proper record of commissions transmitted to that office by the county clerk pursuant to the provisions of this section.

12. Except for changes made in an application for reappointment, the Secretary of State shall receive a non-refundable fee of $10 for changing the name or address of a notary public.

13. The Secretary of State may issue a duplicate identification card to a notary public for one lost, destroyed or damaged upon application therefor on a form prescribed by the Secretary of State and upon payment of a non-refundable fee of $10. Each such duplicate identification card shall have the word "duplicate" stamped across the face thereof, and shall bear the same number as the one it replaces.

§132. Certificates of official character of notaries public.

The Secretary of State or the county clerk of the county in which the commission of a notary public is filed may certify to the official character of such notary public and any notary public may file his autograph signature and a certificate of official character in the office of any county clerk of any county in the State and in any register's office in any county having a register and thereafter such county clerk may certify as to the official character of such notary public. The Secretary of State shall collect for each certificate of official character issued by him the sum of $10. The county clerk and register of any county with whom a certificate of official character has been filed shall collect for filing the same the sum of $10. For each certificate of official character issued, with seal attached, by any county clerk, the sum of $5 shall be collected by him.

§133. Certification of notarial signatures.

The county clerk of a county in whose office any notary public has qualified or has filed his autograph signature and a certificate of his official character, shall, when so requested and upon payment of a fee of $3 affix to any certificate of proof or acknowledgment or oath signed by such notary anywhere in the State of New York, a certificate under his hand and seal, stating that a commission or a certificate of his official character with his autograph signature has been filed in his office, and that he was at the time of taking such proof or acknowledgment or oath duly authorized to take the same; that he is well acquainted with the handwriting of such notary public or has compared the signature on the certificate of proof or acknowledgment or oath with the autograph signature deposited in his office by such notary public and believes that the signature is genuine. An instrument with such certificate of authentication of the county clerk affixed thereto shall be entitled to be read in evidence or to be recorded in any of the counties of this State in respect to which a certificate of a county clerk may be necessary for either purpose.

§140. Executive Law.

14. No person who has been removed from office as a commissioner of deeds for the City of New York, as hereinbefore provided, shall thereafter be eligible again to be appointed as such commissioner nor, shall he be eligible thereafter to appoint to the office of notary public.

15. Any person who has been removed from office as aforesaid, who shall, after knowledge of such removal, sign or execute any instrument as a commissioner of deeds or notary public shall be deemed guilty of a misdemeanor.

§§3-200 and 3-400. Election Law.

A commissioner of elections or inspector of elections is eligible for the office of notary public.

§3. Public Officers Law.

No person is eligible for the office of notary public who has been convicted of a violation of the selective draft act of the U.S. enacted May 18, 1917, or the acts amendatory or supplemental thereto, or of the federal selective training and service act of 1940 or the acts amendatory thereof or supplemental thereto.

§534. County Law.

Each county clerk shall designate from among the members of his or her staff at least one notary public to be available to notarize documents for the public in each county clerk's office during normal business hours free of charge. Each individual appointed by the county clerk to be a notary public pursuant to this section shall be exempt from the examination fee and application fee required by §131 of the Executive Law.

Miscellaneous

Member of legislature.

"If a member of the legislature be * * * appointed to any office, civil * * * under the government * * * the State of New York * * * his or her acceptance thereof shall vacate his or her seat in the legislature, providing, however, that a member of the legislature may be appointed * * * to any office in which he or she shall receive no compensation." (§7 of Article III of the Constitution of the State of New York.) A member of the legislature may be appointed a notary public in view of transfer of power of such appointment from the governor and senate to the Secretary of State. (1927, Op. Atty. Gen. 97.)

Sheriffs.

* * * Sheriffs shall hold no other office. * * * (§13(a) of Article XIII of the Constitution of the State of New York.)

Notary public — disqualifications.

Though a person may be eligible to hold the office of notary the person may be disqualified to act in certain cases by reason of having an interest in the case. To state the rule broadly: if the notary is a party to or directly and pecuniarily interested in the transaction, the person is not capable of acting in that case. For example, a notary who is a grantee or mortgagee in a conveyance or mortgage is disqualified to take the acknowledgment of the grantor or mortgagor; likewise a notary who is a trustee in a deed of trust; and, of course, a notary who is the grantor could not take his own acknowledgment. A notary beneficially interested in the conveyance by way of being secured thereby is not competent to take the acknowledgment of the instrument. In New York the courts have held an acknowledgment taken by a person financially or beneficially interested in a party to conveyance or instrument of which it is a part to be a nullity; and that the acknowledgment of an assignment of a mortgage before one of the assignees is a nullity; and that an acknowledgment by one of the incorporators of the other incorporators who signed a certificate was of no legal effect.

POWERS AND DUTIES

Index

Law	Sec	Subject
Real Property Law	290	Definitions
Real Property Law	298	Acknowledgments and Proofs within the State
Real Property Law	300	Acknowledgments and Proofs by Persons in the U.S. Armed Forces
Real Property Law	302	Acknowledgments and Proofs by Married Women
Real Property Law	303	Requisites of Acknowledgments
Real Property Law	304	Proof by Subscribing Witness
Real Property Law	306	Certificate of Acknowledgment or Proof
Real Property Law	309	Acknowledgment by Corporation
Real Property Law	309-a	Uniform Acknowledgment Certificate, within the State
Real Property Law	309-b	Uniform Acknowledgment Certificate, outside the State
Real Property Law	330	Officers Guilty of Malfeasance
Real Property Law	333	When Conveyances Not to Be Recorded
Banking Law	335	Unpaid Rental of Safe Deposit Box
Civil Practice Law and Rules	3113	Taking of Deposition by Notary
Domestic Relation	11	No Authority to Solemnize Marriage
Public Officers Law	10	Administering Oath of Public Officer

Executive Law

§134. Signature and seal of county clerk.

The signature and seal of a county clerk, upon a certificate of official character of a notary public or the signature of a county clerk upon a certificate of authentication of the signature and acts of a notary public or commissioner of deeds, may be a facsimile, printed, stamped, photographed or engraved thereon.

§135. Powers and duties; in general; of notaries public who are attorneys at law.

Every notary public duly qualified is hereby authorized and empowered within and throughout the State to administer oaths and affirmations, to take affidavits and depositions, to receive and certify acknowledgments or proof of deeds, mortgages and powers of attorney and other instruments in writing; to demand acceptance or payment of foreign and inland bills of exchange, promissory notes and obligations in writing, and to protest the same for non-acceptance or non-payment, as the case may require, and, for use in another jurisdiction, to exercise such other powers and duties as by the laws of nations and according to commercial usage, or by the laws of any other government or country may be exercised and performed by notaries public, provided that when exercising such powers he shall set forth the name of such other jurisdiction.

A notary public who is an attorney at law regularly admitted to practice in this State may, in his discretion, administer an oath or affirmation to or take the affidavit or acknowledgment of his client in respect of any matter, claim, action or proceeding.

For any misconduct by a notary public in the performance of any of his powers such notary public shall be liable to the parties injured for all damages sustained by them. A notary public shall not, directly or indirectly, demand or receive for the protest for the non-payment of any note, or for the non-acceptance or non-payment of any bill of exchange, check or draft and giving the requisite notices and certificates of such protest, including his notarial seal, if affixed thereto, any greater fee or reward than 75 cents for such protest, and 10 cents for each notice, not exceeding five, on any bill or note. Every notary public having a seal shall, except as otherwise provided, and when requested, affix his seal to such protest free of expense.

§135-a. Notary public or commissioner of deeds; acting without appointment; fraud in office.

1. Any person who holds himself out to the public as being entitled to act as a notary public or commissioner of deeds, or who assumes, uses or advertises the title of notary public or commissioner of deeds, or equivalent terms in any language, in such a manner as to convey the impression that he is a notary public or commissioner of deeds without having first been appointed as notary public or commissioner of deeds, or

2. A notary public or commissioner of deeds, who in the exercise of the powers, or in the performance of the duties of such office shall practice any fraud or deceit, the punishment for which is not otherwise provided for by this act, shall be guilty of a misdemeanor.

§135-b. Advertising by notaries public.

1. The provisions of this section shall not apply to attorneys-at-law, admitted to practice in the state of New York.

2. A notary public who advertises his or her services as a notary public in a language other than English shall post with such advertisement a notice in such other language the following statement: "I am not an attorney licensed to practice law and may not give legal advice about immigration or any other legal matter or accept fees for legal advice."

3. A notary public shall not use terms in a foreign language in any advertisement for his or her services as a notary public that mean or imply that the notary public is an attorney licensed to practice in the state of New York or in any jurisdiction of the United States. The secretary shall designate by rule or regulation the terms in a foreign language that shall be deemed to mean or imply that a notary public is licensed to practice law in the state of New York and the use of which shall be prohibited by notary publics who are subject to this section.

4. For purposes of this section, "advertisement" shall mean and include material designed to give notice of or to promote or describe the services offered by a notary public for profit and shall include business cards, brochures, and notices, whether in print or electronic form.

5. Any person who violates any provision of this section or any rule or regulation promulgated by the secretary may be liable for civil penalty of up to one thousand dollars. The secretary of state may suspend a notary public upon a second violation of any of the provisions of this section and may remove from office a notary public upon a third violation of any of the provisions of this section, provided that the notary public shall have been served with a copy of the charges against him or her and been given an opportunity to be heard. The civil penalty provided for by this subdivision shall be recoverable in an action instituted by the attorney general on his or her own initiative or at the request of the secretary.

6. The secretary may promulgate rules and regulations governing the provisions of this section, including the size and type of statements that a notary public is required by this section to post.

§136. Notarial fees.
A notary public shall be entitled to the following fees:

1. For administering an oath or affirmation, and certifying the same when required, except where another fee is specifically prescribed by statute, $2.

2. For taking and certifying the acknowledgment or proof of execution of a written instrument, by one person, $2, and by each additional person, $2, for swearing such witness thereto, $2.

§137. Statement as to authority of notaries public.
In exercising his powers pursuant to this article, a notary public, in addition to the venue of his act and his signature, shall print, typewrite, or stamp beneath his signature in black ink, his name, the words "Notary Public State of New York," the name of the county in which he originally qualified, and the date upon which his commission expires and, in addition, wherever required, a notary public shall also include the name of any county in which his certificate of official character is filed, using the words "Certificate filed _____ County." A notary public who is duly licensed as an attorney and counselor at law in this State may in his discretion, substitute the words "Attorney and Counselor at Law" for the words "Notary Public." A notary public who has qualified or who has filed a certificate of official character in the office of the clerk in a county or counties within the City of New York must also affix to each instrument his official number or numbers in black ink, as given to him by the clerk or clerks of such county or counties at the time such notary qualified in such county or counties and, if the instrument is to be recorded in an office of the register of the City of New York in any county within such city and the notary has been given a number or numbers by such register or his predecessors in any county or counties, when his autographed signature and certificate are filed in such office or offices pursuant to this chapter, he shall also affix such number or numbers. No official act of such notary public shall be held invalid on account of the failure to comply with these provisions. If any notary public shall willfully fail to comply with any of the provisions of this section, he shall be subject to disciplinary action by the secretary of state. In all the courts within this State the certificate of a notary public, over his

signature, shall be received as presumptive evidence of the facts contained in such certificate; provided, that any person interested as a party to a suit may contradict, by other evidence, the certificate of a notary public.

§138. Powers of notaries public or other officers who are stockholders, directors, officers or employees of a corporation.

A notary public, justice of the supreme court, a judge, clerk, deputy clerk, or special deputy clerk of a court, an official examiner of title, or the mayor or recorder of a city, a justice of the peace, surrogate, special surrogate, special county judge, or commissioner of deeds, who is a stockholder, director, officer or employee of a corporation may take the acknowledgment or proof of any party to a written instrument executed to or by such corporation, or administer an oath of any other stockholder, director, officer, employee or agent of such corporation, and such notary public may protest for non- acceptance or non-payment, bills of exchange, drafts, checks, notes and other negotiable instruments owned or held for collection by such corporation; but none of the officers above named shall take the acknowledgment or proof of a written instrument by or to a corporation of which he is a stockholder, director, officer or employee, if such officer taking such acknowledgment or proof to be a party executing such instrument, either individually or as representative of such corporation, nor shall a notary public protest any negotiable instruments owned or held for collection by such corporation, if such notary public be individually a party to such instrument, or have a financial interest in the subject of same. All such acknowledgments or proofs of deeds, mortgages or other written instruments, relating to real property heretofore taken before any of the officers aforesaid are confirmed. This act shall not affect any action or legal proceeding now pending.

§142-a. Validity of acts of notaries public and commissioners of deeds notwithstanding certain defects.

1. Except as provided in subdivision three of this section, the official certificates and other acts heretofore or hereafter made or performed of notaries public and commissioners of deeds heretofore or hereafter and prior to the time of their acts appointed or commissioned as such shall not be deemed invalid, impaired or in any manner defective, so far as they may be affected, impaired or questioned by reason of defects described in subdivision two of this section.

2. This section shall apply to the following defects:

(a) ineligibility of the notary public or commissioner of deeds to be appointed or commissioned as such;

(b) misnomer or misspelling of name or other error made in his appointment or commission;

(c) omission of the notary public or commissioner of deeds to take or file his official oath or otherwise qualify;

(d) expiration of his term, commission or appointment;

(e) vacating of his office by change of his residence, by acceptance of another public office, or by other action on his part;

(f) the fact that the action was taken outside the jurisdiction where the notary public or commissioner of deeds was authorized to act.

3. No person shall be entitled to assert the effect of this section to overcome a defect described in subdivision two if he knew of the defect or if the defect was apparent on the face of the certificate of the notary public or commissioner of deeds; provided however, that this subdivision shall not apply after the expiration of six months from the date of the act of the notary public or commissioner of deeds.

4. After the expiration of six months from the date of the official certificate or other act of the commissioner of deeds, subdivision one of this section shall be applicable to a defect consisting in omission of the certificate of a commissioner of deeds to state the date on which and the place in which an act was done, or consisting of an error in such statement.

5. This section does not relieve any notary public or commissioner of deeds from criminal liability imposed by reason of his act, or enlarge the actual authority of any such officer, nor limit any other statute or rule of law by reason of which the act of a notary public or commissioner of deeds, or the record thereof, is valid or is deemed valid in any case.

Real Property Law
§290. Definitions; effect of article.

* * * 3. The term "conveyance" includes every written instrument, by which any estate or interest in real property is created, transferred, mortgaged or assigned, or by which the title to any real property may be affected, including an instrument in execution of power, although the power be one of revocation only, and an instrument postponing or subordinating a mortgage lien; except a will, a lease for a term not exceeding three years, an executory contract for the sale or purchase of lands, and an instrument containing a power to convey real property as the agent or attorney for the owner of such property. * * *

§298. Acknowledgments and proofs within the state.

The acknowledgment or proof, within this state, of a conveyance of real property situate in this State may be made:

1. At any place within the state, before
(a) a justice of the supreme court;
(b) an official examiner of title;
(c) an official referee; or
(d) a notary public.

2. Within the district wherein such officer is authorized to perform official duties, before
(a) a judge or clerk of any court of record;
(b) a commissioner of deeds outside of the City of New York, or a commissioner of deeds of the City of New York within the five counties comprising the City of New York;
(c) the mayor or recorder of a city;
(d) a surrogate, special surrogate, or special county judge; or
(e) the county clerk or other recording officer of a county.

3. Before a justice of the peace, town councilman, village police justice or a judge of any court of inferior local jurisdiction, anywhere within the county containing the town, village or city in which he is authorized to perform official duties.

§300. Acknowledgments and proofs by persons in or with the armed forces of the United States.

The acknowledgment or proof of a conveyance of real property situated in this state, if made by a person enlisted or commissioned in or serving in or with the armed forces of the United States or by a dependent of any such person, wherever located, or by a person attached to or accompanying the armed forces of the United States, whether made within or without the United States, may be made before any commissioned officer in active service of the armed forces of the United States with the rank of second lieutenant or higher in the Army, Air Force or Marine Corps, or ensign or higher in the Navy or Coast Guard, or with equivalent rank in any other component part of the armed forces of the United States. * * *

The certificate of an acknowledgment or proof taken under this section shall state (a) the rank and serial number of the officer taking the same, and the command to which he is attached, (b) that the person making such acknowledgment or proof was, at the time of making the same, enlisted or commissioned in or serving in or with the armed forces of the United States or the dependent of such a person, or a person attached to or accompanying the armed forces of the United States, and (c) the serial number of the person who makes, or whose dependent makes, the acknowledgment or proof if such person is enlisted or commissioned in the armed forces of the United States. The place where such acknowledgment or proof is taken need not be disclosed. No authentication of the officer's certificate of acknowledgment or proof shall be required. * * *

§302. Acknowledgments and proofs by married women.

The acknowledgment or proof of a conveyance of real property, within the state, or of any other written instrument, may be made by a married woman the same as if unmarried.

§303. Requisites of acknowledgments.

An acknowledgment must not be taken by any officer unless he knows or has satisfactory evidence, that the person making it is the person described in and who executed such instrument.

§304. Proof by subscribing witness.

When the execution of a conveyance is proved by a subscribing witness, such witness must state his own place of residence, and if his place of residence is in a city, the street and street number, if any thereof, and that he knew the person described in and who executed the conveyance. The proof must not be taken unless the officer is personally acquainted with such witness, or has satisfactory evidence that he is the same person, who was a subscribing witness to the conveyance.

§306. Certificate of acknowledgment or proof.

A person taking the acknowledgment or proof of a conveyance must endorse thereupon or attach thereto, a certificate, signed by himself, stating all the matters required to be done, known, or proved on the taking of such acknowledgment or proof; together with the name and substance of the testimony of each witness examined before him, and if a subscribing witness, his place of residence. * * *

§309. Acknowledgment by corporation and form of certificate.

1. The acknowledgment of a conveyance or other instrument by a corporation, must be made by an officer or attorney in fact duly appointed, or in case of a dissolved corporation, by an officer, director or attorney in fact duly appointed thereof authorized to execute the same by the board of directors of said corporation.

2. The certificate of acknowledgment must conform substantially with one of the following alternative forms, the blanks being properly filled:

State of New York)
) ss.:
County of _____)

On the _____ day of _____ in the year _____ before me personally came _____, to me known, who, being by me duly sworn, did depose and say that he/she/they reside(s) in _____ (if the place of residence is in a city, include the street and street number, if any, thereof); that he/she/they is (are) the (president or other officer or director or attorney in fact duly appointed) of the (name of corporation), the corporation described in and which executed the above instrument; that he/she/they know(s) the seal of said corporation; that the seal affixed to said instrument is such corporate seal; that it was so affixed by authority of the board of directors of said corporation, and that he/she/they signed his/her/their name(s) thereto by like authority.

(Signature and office of person taking acknowledgment.)

State of New York)
) ss.:
County of _____)

On the _____ day of _____ in the year _____ before me personally came _____, to me known, who, being by me duly sworn, did depose and say that he/she/they reside(s) in _____ (if the place of residence is in a city, include the street and street number, if any, thereof); that he/she/they is (are) the (president or other officer or director or attorney in fact duly appointed) of the (name of corporation), the corporation described in and which executed the above instrument; and that he/she/they signed his/her/their name(s) thereto by authority of the board of directors of said corporation.

(Signature and office of person taking acknowledgment.)

3. Subdivision two of this section shall be inapplicable to the acknowledgment, within this state, of a conveyance or other instrument in

respect to real property situate in this state executed on or after the first day of September, nineteen hundred ninety-nine. A certificate of such an acknowledgment shall be subject to the provisions of section three hundred nine-a of this article.

§309-a. Uniform forms of certificates of acknowledgment or proof within this state.

1. The certificate of an acknowledgment, within this State, or a conveyance or other instrument in respect to real property situate in this State, by a person, must conform substantially with the following form, the blanks being properly filled:

State of New York)
*   ) ss.:*
County of _____)

On the _____ day of _____ in the year _____ before me, the undersigned, personally appeared _____, personally known to me or proved to me on the basis of satisfactory evidence to be the individual(s) whose name(s) is (are) subscribed to the within instrument and acknowledged to me that he/she/they executed the same in his/her/their capacity(ies), and that by his/her/their signature(s) on the instrument, the individual(s), or the person upon behalf of which the individual(s) acted, executed the instrument.

(Signature and office of individual taking acknowledgment.)

2. The certificate for a proof of execution by a subscribing witness, within this state, of a conveyance or other instrument made by any person in respect to real property situate in this state, must conform substantially with the following form, the blanks being properly filled:

State of New York)
*   ) ss.:*
County of _____)

On the _____ day of _____ in the year _____ before me, the undersigned, personally appeared _____, the subscribing witness to the foregoing instrument, with whom I am personally acquainted, who, being by me duly sworn, did depose and say that he/she/they reside(s) in _____ (if the place of residence is in a city, include the street and street number, if any, thereof); that he/she/they know(s) _____ to be the individual described in and who executed the foregoing instrument; that said subscribing witness was present and saw said _____ execute the same; and that said witness at the same time subscribed his/her/their name(s) as a witness thereto.

(Signature and office of individual taking proof).

3. A certificate of an acknowledgment or proof taken under §300 of this article shall include the additional information required by that section.
4. For the purposes of this section, the term "person" means any

corporation, joint stock company, estate, general partnership (including any registered limited liability partnership or foreign limited liability partnership), limited liability company (including a professional service limited liability company), foreign limited liability company (including a foreign professional service limited liability company), joint venture, limited partnership, natural person, attorney in fact, real estate investment trust, business trust or other trust, custodian, nominee or any other individual or entity in its own or any representative capacity.

§309-b. Uniform forms of certificates of acknowledgment or proof without this state.

1. The certificate of an acknowledgment, without this State, of a conveyance or other instrument with respect to real property situate in this State, by a person, may conform substantially with the following form, the blanks being properly filled:

State, District of Columbia,)
Territory, Possession, or) *ss.:*
Foreign Country _____)

On the _____ day of _____ in the year _____ before me, the undersigned, personally appeared _____, personally known to me or proved to me on the basis of satisfactory evidence to be the individual(s) whose name(s) is (are) subscribed to the within instrument and acknowledged to me that he/she/ they executed the same in his/her/their capacity(ies), and that by his/her/their signature(s) on the instrument, the individual(s), or the person upon behalf of which the individual(s) acted, executed the instrument.

(Signature and office of individual taking acknowledgment.)

2. The certificate for a proof of execution by a subscribing witness, without this State, of a conveyance or other instrument made by any person in respect to real property situate in this State, may conform substantially with the following form, the blanks being properly filled:

State, District of Columbia,)
Territory, Possession, or) *ss.:*
Foreign Country _____)

On the _____ day of _____ in the year _____ before me, the undersigned, personally appeared _____, the subscribing witness to the foregoing instrument, with whom I am personally acquainted, who, being by me duly sworn, did depose and say that he/she resides in _____ (if the place of residence is in a city, include the street and street number, if any, thereof); that he/she knows _____ to be the individual described in and who executed the foregoing instrument; that said subscribing witness was present and saw said _____ execute the same; and that said witness at the same time subscribed his/her name as a witness thereto.

(Signature and office of individual taking proof.)

3. No provision of this section shall be construed to:

(a) modify the choice of laws afforded by §§299-a and 301-a of this article pursuant to which an acknowledgment or proof may be taken;

(b) modify any requirement of §307 of this article;

(c) modify any requirement for a seal imposed by subdivision one of §308 of this article;

(d) modify any requirement concerning a certificate of authentication imposed by §308, 311, 312, 314, or 318 of this article; or

(e) modify any requirement imposed by any provision of this article when the certificate of acknowledgment or proof purports to be taken in the manner prescribed by the laws of another state, the District of Columbia, territory, possession, or foreign country.

4. A certificate of an acknowledgment or proof taken under §300 of this article shall include the additional information required by that section.

5. For the purposes of this section, the term "person" means a person as defined in subdivision 4 of §309-a of this article.

6. The inclusion within the body (other than the jurat) of a certificate of acknowledgment or proof made under this section or the city or other political subdivision and the state or country or other place the acknowledgment was taken shall be deemed. A non-substantial variance from the form of a certificate authorized by this section.

§330. Officers guilty of malfeasance liable for damages.

An officer authorized to take the acknowledgment or proof of a conveyance or other instrument, or to certify such proof or acknowledgment, or to record the same, who is guilty of malfeasance or fraudulent practice in the execution of any duty prescribed by law in relation thereto, is liable in damages to the person injured.

§333. When conveyances of real property not to be recorded.

* * * 2. A recording officer shall not record or accept for record any conveyance of real property, unless said conveyance in its entirety and the certificate of acknowledgment or proof and the authentication thereof, other than proper names therein which may be in another language provided they are written in English letters or characters, shall be in the English language, or unless such conveyance, certificate of acknowledgment or proof, and the authentication thereof be accompanied by and have attached thereto a translation in the English language duly executed and acknowledged by the person or persons making such conveyance and proved and authenticated, if need be, in the manner required of conveyances for recording in this state, or, unless such conveyance, certificate of acknowledgment or proof, and the authentication thereof be accompanied by and have attached thereto a translation in the English language made by a person duly designated for such purpose by the county judge of the county where it is desired to record such conveyance or a justice of the supreme court and be duly signed, acknowledged and certified under oath or upon affirmation by such person before such judge, to be a true and accurate translation and contain a certification of the designation of such person by such judge.

Special Note

By reason of changes in certain provisions of the Real Property Law, any and all limitations on the authority of a notary public to act as such in any part of the State have been removed; a notary public may now, in addition to administering oaths or taking affidavits anywhere in the State, take acknowledgments and proofs of conveyances anywhere in the State. The need for a certificate of authentication of a county clerk as a prerequisite to recording or use in evidence in this State of the instrument acknowledged or proved has been abolished. The certificate of authentication may possibly be required where the instrument is to be recorded or used in evidence outside the jurisdiction of the State.

§335. Banking Law

If the rental fee of any safe deposit box is not paid, or after the termination of the lease for such box, and at least 30 days after giving proper notice to the lessee, the lessor (bank) may, in the presence of a notary public, open the safe deposit box, remove and inventory the contents. The notary public shall then file with the lessor a certificate under seal which states the date of the opening of the safe deposit box, the name of the lessee, and a list of the contents. Within 10 days of the opening of the safe deposit box, a copy of this certificate must be mailed to the lessee at his last known postal address.

Rule 3113. Civil Practice Law and Rules

This rule authorizes a deposition to be taken before a notary public in a civil proceeding.

§11. Domestic Relations Law

A notary public has no authority to solemnize marriages; nor may a notary public take the acknowledgment of parties and witnesses to a written contract of marriage.

§10. Public Officers Law

Official oaths, permits the oath of a public officer to be administered by a notary public.

RESTRICTIONS AND VIOLATIONS

Index

Law	Sec	Subject
Judiciary Law	484	None but Attorneys to Practice
Judiciary Law	485	Misdemeanor Violations
Judiciary Law	750	Powers of Courts to Punish
Public Officers Law	15	Notary Must Not Act Before Taking/Filing Oath
Public Officers Law	67	Fees of Public Officers
Public Officers Law	69	Fees Prohibited for Administering Certain Oaths
Executive Law		Removal From Office for Misconduct

Penal Law	70.00	Sentence of Imprisonment for Felony
Penal Law	70.15	Sentences of Imprisonment for Misdemeanors
Penal Law	170.10	Forgery in the Second Degree
Penal Law	175.40	Issuing a False Certificate
Penal Law	195.00	Official Misconduct

Judiciary Law
§484. None but attorneys to practice in the state.

No natural person shall ask or receive, directly or indirectly, compensation for appearing for a person other than himself as attorney in any court or before any magistrate, or for preparing deeds, mortgages, assignments, discharges, leases or any other instruments affecting real estate, wills, codicils, or any other instrument affecting the disposition of property after death, or decedents' estates, or pleadings of any kind in any action brought before any court of record in this state, or make it a business to practice for another as an attorney in any court or before any magistrate unless he has been regularly admitted to practice, as an attorney or counselor, in the courts of record in the state; but nothing in this section shall apply:

1. to officers of societies for the prevention of cruelty, duly appointed, when exercising the special powers conferred upon such corporations under §1403 of the Not-for-Profit Corporation Law; or

2. to law students who have completed at least 2 semesters of law school or persons who have graduated from a law school, who have taken the examination for admittance to practice law in the courts of record in the state immediately available after graduation from law school, or the examination immediately available after being notified by the board of law examiners that they failed to pass said exam, and who have not been notified by the board of law examiners that they have failed to pass two such examinations, acting under the supervision of a legal aid organization, when such students and persons are acting under a program approved by the appellate division of the supreme court of the department in which the principal office of such organization is located and specifying the extent to which such students and persons may engage in activities prohibited by this statute; or

3. to persons who have graduated from a law school approved pursuant to the rules of the court of appeals for the admission of attorneys and counselors-at-law and who have taken the examination for admission to practice as an attorney and counselor-at-law immediately available after graduation from law school or the examination immediately available after being notified by the board of law examiners that they failed to pass said exam, and who have not been notified by the board of law examiners that they have failed to pass two such examinations, when such persons are acting under the supervision of the state or a subdivision thereof or of any officer or agency of the state or a subdivision thereof, pursuant to a program approved by the appellate division of the supreme court of the department within which such activities are taking place and specifying the extent to which they may engage in activities otherwise prohibited by this statute and those powers of the supervising governmental entity or officer

in connection with which they may engage in such activities.

§485. Violation of certain preceding sections a misdemeanor.

Any person violating the provisions of §§478, 479, 480, 481, 482, 483 or 484, shall be guilty of a misdemeanor.

§750. Power of courts to punish for criminal contempts.

* * * B. * * * the supreme court has power under this section to punish for a criminal contempt any person who unlawfully practices or assumes to practice law; and a proceeding under this subdivision may be instituted on the court's own motion or on the motion of any officer charged with the duty of investigating or prosecuting unlawful practice of law, or by any bar association incorporated under the laws of this State.

Illegal practice of law by notary public.

To make it a business to practice as an attorney at law, not being a lawyer, is a crime. "Counsel and advice, the drawing of agreements, the organization of corporations and preparing papers connected therewith, the drafting of legal documents of all kinds, including wills, are activities which have been long classed as law practice." (*People v. Alfani*, 227 NY 334, 339.)

Wills.

The execution of wills under the supervision of a notary public acting in effect as a lawyer, "cannot be too strongly condemned, not only for the reason that it means an invasion of the legal profession, but for the fact that testators thereby run the risk of frustrating their own solemnly declared intentions and rendering worthless maturely considered plans for the disposition of estates whose creation may have been the fruit of lives of industry and self-denial." (*Matter of Flynn*, 142 Misc. 7.)

Public Officers Law

Notary must not act before taking and filing oath of office.

The Public Officers Law (§15) provides that a person who executes any of the functions of a public office without having taken and duly filed the required oath of office, as prescribed by law, is guilty of a misdemeanor. A notary public is a public officer.

§67. Fees of public officers.

1. Each public officer upon whom a duty is expressly imposed by law, must execute the same without fee or reward, except where a fee or other compensation therefor is expressly allowed by law.

2. An officer or other person, to whom a fee or other compensation is allowed by law, for any service, shall not charge or receive a greater fee or reward, for that service, than is so allowed.

3. An officer, or other person, shall not demand or receive any fee or compensation, allowed to him by law for any service, unless the service was actually rendered by him; except that an officer may demand in advance his fee, where he is, by law, expressly directed or permitted to require payment thereof, before rendering the service.

4. * * * An officer or other person, who violates either of the provisions contained in this section, is liable, in addition to the punishment prescribed by law for the criminal offense, to an action in behalf of the person aggrieved, in which the plaintiff is entitled to treble damages.

A notary public subjects himself to criminal prosecution, civil suit and possible removal by asking or receiving more than the statutory allowance, for administering the ordinary oath in connect [sic] with an affidavit. (Op. Atty. Gen. (1917) 12 St. Dept. Rep. 507.)

§69. Fee for administering certain official oaths prohibited.

An officer is not entitled to a fee, for administering the oath of office to a member of the legislature, to any military officer, to an inspector of election, clerk of the poll, or to any other public officer or public employee.

Executive Law
Misconduct by a notary and removal from office.

A notary public who, in the performance of the duties of such office shall practice any fraud or deceit, is guilty of a misdemeanor (Executive Law, §135-a), and may be removed from office. The notary may be removed from office if the notary made a misstatement of a material fact in his application for appointment; for preparing and taking an oath of an affiant to a statement that the notary knew to be false or fraudulent.

Penal Law
§70.00 Sentence of imprisonment for felony.

* * * 2. Maximum term of sentence. The maximum term of an indeterminate sentence shall be at least three years and the term shall be fixed as follows:

* * * (d) For a class D felony, the term shall be fixed by the court, and shall not exceed 7 years; and

(e) For a class E felony, the term shall be fixed by the court, and shall not exceed 4 years. * * *

§70.15 Sentences of imprisonment for misdemeanors and violation.

1. Class A misdemeanor. A sentence of imprisonment for a class A misdemeanor shall be a definite sentence. When such a sentence is imposed the term shall be fixed by the court, and shall not exceed one year; * * *

§80.00 Fine for felony.

1. A sentence to pay a fine for a felony shall be a sentence to pay an amount, fixed by the court, not exceeding the higher of

(a) five thousand dollars; or

(b) double the amount of the defendant's gain from the commission of the crime; * * *

When imposing a fine pursuant to the provisions of this paragraph, the court shall consider the profit gained by defendant's conduct, whether the amount of the fine is disproportionate to the conduct in which defendant engaged, its impact on any victims, and defendant's economic circumstances, including the defendant's ability to pay, the effect of the fine upon his or her immediate family or any other persons to whom the defendant owes an obligation of support.

2. As used in this section the term "gain" means the amount of money or the value of property derived from the commission of the crime, less the amount of money or the value of property returned to the victim of the crime or seized by or surrendered to lawful authority prior to the time sentence is imposed.

3. When the court imposes a fine for a felony pursuant to paragraph b of subdivision one of this section, the court shall make a finding as to the amount of the defendant's gain from the crime. If the record does not contain sufficient evidence to support such a finding * * *, the court may conduct a hearing upon such issues. * * *

§80.05 Fines for misdemeanors and violation.

1. Class A misdemeanor. A sentence to pay a fine for a class A misdemeanor shall be a sentence to pay an amount, fixed by the court, not exceeding one thousand dollars, provided, however, that a sentence imposed for a violation of section 215.80 of this chapter may include a fine in an amount equivalent to double the value of the property unlawfully disposed of in the commission of the crime.

2. Class B misdemeanor. A sentence to pay a fine for a class B misdemeanor shall be a sentence to pay an amount, fixed by the court, not exceeding five hundred dollars.

3. Unclassified misdemeanor. A sentence to pay a fine for an unclassified misdemeanor shall be a sentence to pay an amount, fixed by the court, in accordance with the provisions of the law or ordinance that defines the crime.

4. Violation. A sentence to pay a fine for a violation shall be a sentence to pay an amount, fixed by the court, not exceeding two hundred fifty dollars. In the case of a violation defined outside this chapter, if the amount of the fine is expressly specified in the law or ordinance that defines the offense, the amount of the fine shall be fixed in accordance with that law or ordinance.

5. Alternative sentence. If a person has gained money or property through the commission of any misdemeanor or violation then upon conviction thereof, the court, in lieu of imposing the fine authorized for the offense under one of the above subdivisions, may sentence the defendant to pay an amount, fixed by the court, not exceeding double the amount of the defendant's gain from the commission of the offense; provided, however, that the amount fixed by the court pursuant to this subdivision upon a conviction under section 11-1904 of the environmental conservation law shall not exceed five thousand dollars. In such event the provisions of subdivisions two and three of section 80.00 shall be applicable to the sentence. * * *

§170.10 Forgery in the second degree.

A person is guilty of forgery in the second degree when, with intent to defraud, deceive or injure another, he falsely makes, completes or alters a written instrument which is or purports to be, or which is calculated to become or to represent if completed:

1. A deed, will, codicil, contract, assignment, commercial instrument, or other instrument which does or may evidence, create, transfer, terminate or otherwise affect a legal right, interest, obligation or status; or

2. A public record, or an instrument filed or required or authorized by law to be filed in or with a public office or public servant; or

3. A written instrument officially issued or created by a public office, public servant or governmental instrumentality.

* * * Forgery in the second degree is a class D felony.

§175.40 Issuing a false certificate.

A person is guilty of issuing a false certificate when, being a public servant authorized by law to make or issue official certificates or other official written instruments, and with intent to defraud, deceive or injure another person, he issues such an instrument, or makes the same with intent that it be issued, knowing that it contains a false statement or false information.

Issuing a false certificate is a class E felony.

§195.00 Official misconduct.

A public servant is guilty of official misconduct when, with intent to obtain a benefit or to injure or deprive another person of a benefit:

1. He commits an act relating to his office but constituting an unauthorized exercise of his official functions, knowing that such act is unauthorized; or

2. He knowingly refrains from performing a duty which is imposed upon him by law or is clearly inherent in the nature of his office.

Official misconduct is a class A misdemeanor.

Notary must officiate on request.

The Penal Law (§195.00) provides that an officer before whom an oath or affidavit may be taken is bound to administer the same when requested, and a refusal to do so is a misdemeanor. (*People v. Brooks*, 1 Den. 457.)

Perjury.

One is guilty of perjury if he has stated or given testimony on a material matter, under oath or by affirmation, as to the truth thereof, when he knew the statement or testimony to be false and willfully made.

DEFINITIONS AND GENERAL TERMS

Acknowledgment. A formal declaration before a duly authorized officer by a person who has executed an instrument that such execution is his act and deed.

Technically, an "acknowledgment" is the declaration of a person described in and who has executed a written instrument, that he executed the same. As commonly used, the term means the certificate of an officer, duly empowered to take an acknowledgment or proof of the conveyance of real property, that **on a specified date "before me came _____, to me known to be the individual described in and who executed the foregoing instrument and acknowledged that he executed the**

same." The purposes of the law respecting acknowledgments are not only to promote the security of land titles and to prevent frauds in conveyancing, but to furnish proof of the due execution of conveyances (*Armstrong v. Combs*, 15 App. Div. 246) so as to permit the document to be given in evidence, without further proof of its execution, and make it a recordable instrument.

The Real Property Law prescribes:

"**§303. Requisites of acknowledgments.** An acknowledgment must not be taken by any officer unless he knows or has satisfactory evidence, that the person making it is the person described in and who executed such instrument."

The thing to be known is the identity of the person making the acknowledgment with the person described in the instrument and the person who executed the same. This knowledge must be possessed by the notary (*Gross v. Rowley*, 147 App. Div. 529), and a notary must not take an acknowledgment unless the notary knows or has proof that the person making it is the person described in and who executed the instrument (*People v. Kempner*, 49 App. Div. 121). It is not essential that the person who executed the instrument sign his name in the presence of the notary.

Taking acknowledgments over the telephone is illegal and a notary public is guilty of a misdemeanor in so acting. **In the certificate of acknowledgment a notary public declares: "On this _____ day of _____, 20___, before me came_____, to me known,"** etc. Unless the person purporting to have made the acknowledgment actually and personally appeared before the notary on the day specified, the notary's certificate that he so came is palpably false and fraudulent. (*Matter of Brooklyn Bar Assoc.*, 225 App. Div. 680.)

Interest as a disqualification. A notary public should not take an acknowledgment to a legal instrument to which the notary is a party in interest. (*Armstrong v. Combs*, 15 App. Div. 246.)

Fraudulent certificates of acknowledgment. A notary public who knowingly makes a false certificate that a deed or other written instrument was acknowledged by a party thereto is guilty of forgery in the second degree, which is punishable by imprisonment for a term of not exceeding 7 years (Penal Law, §§170.10 and 70.00[2(d)]. The essence of the crime is false certification, intention to defraud. (*People v. Abeel*, 182 NY 415.) While the absence of guilty knowledge or criminal intent would absolve the notary from criminal liability, the conveyance, of which the false certification is an essential part, is a forgery and, therefore, invalid. (*Caccioppoli v. Lemmo*, 152 App. Div. 650.)

Damages recoverable from notary for false certificate. Action for damages sustained where notary certified that mortgagor had appeared and acknowledged a mortgage. (*Kainz v. Goldsmith*, 231 App. Div. 171.)

Administrator. A person appointed by the court to manage the estate of a deceased person who left no will.

Affiant. The person who makes and subscribes his signature to an affidavit.

Affidavit. An affidavit is a signed statement, duly sworn to, by the maker thereof, before a notary public or other officer authorized to administer oaths. The venue, or county wherein the affidavit was sworn to should be accurately stated. But it is of far more importance that the affiant, the person making the affidavit, should have personally appeared before the notary and have made oath to the statements contained in the affidavit as required by law. Under the Penal Law (§210.00) the willful making of a false affidavit is perjury, but to sustain an indictment therefor, there must have been, in some form, in the presence of an officer authorized to administer an oath, an unequivocal and present act by which the affiant consciously took upon himself the obligation of an oath; his silent delivery of a signed affidavit to the notary for his certificate, is not enough. (*People v. O'Reilly*, 86 NY 154; People ex rel. *Greene v. Swasey*, 122 Misc. 388; *People v. Levitas* [1963] 40 Misc. 2d 331.) A notary public will be removed from office for preparing and taking the oath of an affiant to a statement that the notary knew to be false. (*Matter of Senft*, August 8, 1929; *Matter of Trotta*, February 20, 1930; *Matter of Kibbe*, December 24, 1931.)

The distinction between the taking of an acknowledgment and an affidavit must be clearly understood. In the case of an acknowledgment, the notary public certifies as to the identity and execution of a document; the affidavit involves the administration of an oath to the affiant. There are certain acknowledgment forms which are a combination of an acknowledgment and affidavit. It is incumbent on the notary public to scrutinize each document presented to him and to ascertain the exact nature of the notary's duty with relation thereto. An affidavit differs from a deposition in that an affidavit is an ex parte statement. (*See definition of Deposition.*)

Affirmation. A solemn declaration made by persons who conscientiously decline taking an oath; it is equivalent to an oath and is just as binding; if a person has religious or conscientious scruples against taking an oath, the notary public should have the person affirm. **The following is a form of affirmation: "Do you solemnly, sincerely, and truly, declare and affirm that the statements made by you are true and correct?"**

Apostille. Department of State authentication attached to a notarized and county-certified document for possible international use.

Attest. To witness the execution of a written instrument, at the request of the person who makes it, and subscribe the same as a witness.

Attestation Clause. That clause (e.g., at the end of a will) wherein the witnesses certify that the instrument has been executed before them, and the manner of the execution of the same.

Authentication (Notarial). A certificate subjoined by a county clerk to any certificate of proof or acknowledgment or oath signed by a notary; this county clerk's certificate authenticates or verifies the authority of the notary public to act as such. (See §133, Executive Law.)

Bill of Sale. A written instrument given to pass title of personal property from vendor to vendee.

Certified Copy. A copy of a public record signed and certified as a true copy by the public official having custody of the original. A notary public has no authority to issue certified copies. Notaries must not certify to the authenticity of legal documents and other papers required to be filed with foreign consular officers. Within this prohibition are certificates of the following type:

United States of America   )
State of New York   ) ss.:
County of New York   )

I, _____, a notary public of the State of New York, in and for the county of _____ , duly commissioned, qualified and sworn according to the laws of the State of New York, do hereby certify and declare that I verily believe the annexed instrument executed by _____, and sworn to before _____, a notary public of the State of _____, to be genuine in every respect, and that full faith and credit are and ought to be given thereto.

In testimony whereof I have hereunto set my hand and seal at the City of_____ , this _____ day of _____, 20 _____.

(Seal)   *(Notarial Signature)*

Chattel. Personal property, such as household goods or fixtures.

Chattel Paper. A writing or writings which evidence both an obligation to pay money and a security interest in a lease or specific goods. The agreement which creates or provides for the security interest is known as a security agreement.

Codicil. An instrument made subsequent to a will and modifying it in some respects.

Consideration. Anything of value given to induce entering into a contract; it may be money, personal services, or even love and affection.

Contempt of Court. Behavior disrespectful of the authority of a court which disrupts the execution of court orders.

Contract. An agreement between competent parties to do or not to do certain things for a legal consideration, whereby each party acquires a right to what the other possesses.

Conveyance (Deed). Every instrument, in writing, except a will, by which any estate or interest in real property is created, transferred, assigned or surrendered.

County Clerk's Certificate. See "Authentication (Notarial)."

Deponent. One who makes oath to a written statement. Technically, a person subscribing a deposition but used interchangeably with "Affiant."

Deposition. The testimony of a witness taken out of court or other hearing proceeding, under oath or by affirmation, before a notary public or other person, officer or commissioner before whom such testimony is authorized by law to be taken, which is intended to be used at the trial or hearing.

Duress. Unlawful constraint exercised upon a person whereby he is forced to do some act against his will.

Escrow. The placing of an instrument in the hands of a person as a depository who on the happening of a designated event, is to deliver the instrument to a third person. This agreement, once established, should be unalterable.

Executor. One named in a will to carry out the provisions of the will.

Ex Parte (From One Side Only). A hearing or examination in the presence of, or on papers filed by, one party and in the absence of the other.

Felony. A crime punishable by death or imprisonment in a state prison.

Guardian. A person in charge of a minor's person or property.

Judgment. Decree of a court declaring that one individual is indebted to another and fixing the amount of such indebtedness.

Jurat. A jurat is that part of an affidavit where the officer (notary public) certifies that it was sworn to before him. It is not the affidavit.
The following is the form of jurat generally employed: **"Sworn to before me this _____ day of _____, 20 ____."**
Those words placed directly after the signature in the affidavit stating that the facts therein contained were sworn to or affirmed before the officer (notary public) together with his official signature and such other data as required by §137 of the Executive Law.

Laches. The delay or negligence in asserting one's legal rights.

Lease. A contract whereby, for a consideration, usually termed rent, one who is entitled to the possession of real property transfers such right to another for life, for a term of years or at will.

Lien. A legal right or claim upon a specific property which attaches to the property until a debt is satisfied.

Litigation. The act of carrying on a lawsuit.

Misdemeanor. Any crime other than a felony.

Mortgage on Real Property. An instrument in writing, duly executed and delivered that creates a lien upon real estate as security for the payment of a specified debt, which is usually in the form of a bond.

Notary Public. A public officer who executes acknowledgments of deeds or writings in order to render them available as evidence of the facts therein contained; administers oaths and affirmation as to the truth of statements contained in papers or documents requiring the administration of an oath. The notary's general authority is defined in §135 of the Executive Law; the notary has certain other powers which can be found in the various provisions of law set forth earlier in this publication.

Oath. A verbal pledge given by the person taking it that his statements are made under an immediate sense of this responsibility to God, who will punish the affiant if the statements are false.

Notaries public must administer oaths and affirmations in manner and form as prescribed by the Civil Practice Law and Rules, namely:

§2309(b) Form. An oath or affirmation shall be administered in a form calculated to awaken the conscience and impress the mind of the person taking it in accordance with his religious or ethical beliefs.

An oath must be administered as required by law. The person taking the oath must personally appear before the notary; an oath cannot be administered over the telephone (*Matter of Napolis*, 169 App. Div. 469), and the oath must be administered in the form required by the statute (*Bookman v. City of New York*, 200 NY 53, 56).

When an oath is administered the person taking the oath must express assent to the oath repeated by the notary by the words "I do" or some other words of like meaning.

For an oath or affirmation to be valid, whatever form is adopted, it is necessary that: first, the person swearing or affirming must personally be in the presence of the notary public; secondly, that the person unequivocally swears or affirms that what he states is true; thirdly, that he swears or affirms as of that time; and, lastly, that the person conscientiously takes upon himself the obligation of an oath.

A notary public does not fulfill his duty by merely asking a person whether the signature on a purported affidavit is his. An oath must be administered.

A corporation or a partnership cannot take an oath; an oath must be taken by an individual.

A notary public cannot administer an oath to himself.

The privileges and rights of a notary public are personal and cannot be delegated to anyone.

Plaintiff. A person who starts a suit or brings an action against another.

Power of Attorney. A written statement by an individual giving another person the power to act for him.

Proof. The formal declaration made by a subscribing witness to the execution of an instrument setting forth his place of residence, that he knew the person described in and who executed the instrument and that he saw such person execute such instrument.

Protest. A formal statement in writing by a notary public, under seal, that a certain bill of exchange or promissory note was on a certain day presented for payment, or acceptance, and that such payment or acceptance was refused.

Seal. The laws of the State of New York do not require the use of seals by notaries public. If a seal is used, it should sufficiently identify the notary public, his authority and jurisdiction. It is the opinion of the Department of State that the only inscription required is the name of the notary and the words "Notary Public State of New York."

Signature of Notary Public. A notary public must sign the name under which he was appointed and no other. In addition to his signature and venue, the notary public shall print, typewrite or stamp beneath his signature in black ink, his name, the words "Notary Public State of New York," the name of the county in which he is qualified, and the date upon which his commission expires (§137, Executive Law).

When a woman notary marries during the term of office for which she was appointed, she may continue to use her maiden name as notary public. However, if she elects to use her marriage name, then for the balance of her term as a notary public she must continue to use her maiden name in her signature and seal when acting in her notarial capacity, adding after her signature her married name, in parentheses. When renewing her commission as a notary public, she may apply under her married name or her maiden name. She must then perform all her notarial functions under the name selected.

A member of a religious order, known therein by a name other than his secular cognomen, may be appointed and may officiate as a notary public under the name by which he is known in religious circles. (Op. Atty. Gen., Mar. 20, 1930.)

Statute. A law established by an act of the Legislature.

Statute of Frauds. State law which provides that certain contracts must be in writing or partially complied with, in order to be enforceable at law.

Statute of Limitations. A law that limits the time within which a criminal prosecution or a civil action must be started.

Subordination Clause. A clause which permits the placing of a mortgage at a later date which takes priority over an existing mortgage.

Sunday. A notary public may administer an oath or take an affidavit or acknowledgment on Sunday. However, a deposition cannot be taken on Sunday in a civil proceeding.

Swear. This term includes every mode authorized by law for administering an oath.

Taking an Acknowledgment. The act of the person named in an instrument telling the notary public that he is the person named in the instrument and acknowledging that he executed such instrument; also includes the act of the notary public in obtaining satisfactory evidence of the identity of the person whose acknowledgment is taken.

The notary public "certifies to the taking of the acknowledgment" when the notary signs his official signature to the form setting forth the fact of the taking of the acknowledgment.

Venue. The geographical place where a notary public takes an affidavit or acknowledgment. Every affidavit or certificate of acknowledgment should show on its face the venue of the notarial act. The venue is usually set forth at the beginning of the instrument or at the top of the notary's jurat, or official certification, as follows: "State of New York, County of (New York) ss.:". Section 137 of the Executive Law imposes the duty on the notary public to include the venue of his act in all certificates of acknowledgments or jurats to affidavits.

Will. The disposition of one's property to take effect after death.

SCHEDULE OF FEES

Appointment as Notary Public — Total Commission Fee	$60.00
($40 appointment and $20 filing of Oath of Office)	
Change of Name/Address	10.00
Duplicate Identification Card	10.00
Issuance of Certificate of Official Character	5.00
Filing Certificate of Official Character	10.00
Authentication Certificate	3.00
Protest of Note, Commercial Paper, etc.	0.75
Each additional Notice of Protest (limit 5) each	0.10
Oath or Affirmation	2.00
Acknowledgment (each person)	2.00
Proof of Execution (each person)	2.00
Swearing Witness	2.00

Note: Where gender pronouns appear in this booklet, they are meant to refer to both male and female persons.

NEW YORK STATE
GENERAL BUSINESS LAW

Article 28-C. Immigrant Assistance Services.
§460-a. Definitions.

1."Immigrant assistance service" means providing assistance, for a fee or other compensation, to persons who have, or plan to, come to the United States from a foreign country, or their representatives, in relation to any proceeding, filing or action affecting the non-immigrant, immigrant or citizenship status of a person which arises under the immigration and nationality law, executive order or presidential proclamation, or which arises under actions or regulations of the United States bureau of citizenship and immigration services, the United States department of labor, or the United States department of state.

§460-b. Immigrant assistance service contracts.

No immigrant assistance service shall be provided until the customer has executed a written contract with the provider who will provide such services. The written contract * * * shall include the following: * * *

7. A statement that the immigration services provider has financial surety in effect for the benefit of any customer in the event that the customer is owed a refund, or is damaged by the actions of the provider, together with the name, address and telephone number of the surety.

§460-e. Prohibited acts.

No provider shall: * * *

2. Assume, use or advertise the title of lawyer or attorney at law, or equivalent terms in the English language or any other language, or represent or advertise other titles or credentials, including but not limited to "notary public", "accredited representative of the board of immigration appeals" or "immigration consultant," that could cause a customer to believe that the person possesses special professional skills or is authorized to provide advice on an immigration matter; provided that a notary public licensed by the secretary of state may use the term "notary public."

NEW YORK CODES, RULES AND REGULATIONS
TITLE 9. EXECUTIVE DEPARTMENT
SUBTITLE N. OFFICE FOR TECHNOLOGY
PART 540. ELECTRONIC SIGNATURES AND RECORDS ACT

Section 540.7. Electronic recording of instruments affecting real property.
***

(e) A notary shall perform a notarization of an instrument affecting real property that exists as an electronic record only where the signatory appears in person before the notary at the time of notarization to execute the record or to affirm a prior execution, as permitted by New York State law. The methods that a notary uses to identify a signatory shall be as prescribed by New York State law. Electronic signatures used by a notary on an instrument affecting real property shall comply with section 291-i (c) of the Real Property Law, and shall be:

(1) unique to the notary;

(2) capable of independent verification;

(3) under the notary's sole control;

(4) attached to, or logically associated with, the electronic record in such a manner that it can be determined if any data contained in the electronic record has been changed subsequent to the electronic notarization; and

***

TITLE 19. DEPARTMENT OF STATE
CHAPTER V. DIVISION OF LICENSING SERVICES
SUBCHAPTER L. NOTARIES PUBLIC
PART 200. NOTARIES PUBLIC

§200.1 Advertising

(a) A notary public who is not an attorney licensed to practice law in the State of New York shall not falsely advertise that he or she is an attorney licensed to practice law in the State of New York or in any jurisdiction of the United States by using foreign terms including, but not limited to: abogado, mandataire, procuratore, Адвокат, 律師, and avoca.

(b) A notary public who is not an attorney licensed to practice law in the State of New York and who advertises his or her services as a notary public in a language other than English shall include in the advertisement the following disclaimer: "I am not an attorney licensed to practice law and may not give legal advice about immigration or any other legal matter or accept fees for legal advice." The disclaimer shall be printed clearly and conspicuously and shall be made in the same language as the advertisement. The translated disclaimer, in some but not all languages, is as follows:

(1) Simplified Chinese:

我不是有执照的律师，不能出庭辩护，不能提供有关移民事务或其他法律事务的法律建议，也不能收取法律咨询的费用。

(2) Traditional Chinese:

本人不是持牌執業律師，因此不能出庭辯護，不能向閣下提供移民及其他法律事務方面的法律意見，也不能收取法律諮詢費

(3) Spanish:

"No estoy facultado para ejercer la profesión de abogado y no puedo brindar asesoría legal sobre inmigración o ningún otro asunto legal como tampoco puedo cobrar honorarios por la asesoría legal."

(4) Korean:

저는 법을 집행할 수 있는 자격이 있는 변호사가 아니며, 이민이나 또는 다른 적법한 문제나 혹은 적법한 조언에 대한 수수료를 받을 수 있는지에 대한 법률상의 조언을 드릴수 가 없을지도 모릅니다.

(5) Haitian Creole:

MWEN PA AVOKA KI GEN LISANS POU PRATIKE LWA E MWEN PA KA BAY KONSÈY LEGAL SOU ZAFÈ IMIGRASYON OSWA NENPÒT KI LÒT ZAFÈ LEGAL OSWA AKSEPTE LAJEN POU BAY KONSÈY LEGAL." ■

Offices of the New York Department of State

The following offices of the New York Department of State's Division of Licensing Services may provide applications for Notary Public appointments. All first-time applications must be mailed to the Albany office. Applications for renewal are processed through the local county clerk's office.

Albany
New York Department of State
Division of Licensing Services
Alfred E. Smith Office Bldg.
80 South Swan Street, 10th Floor
Albany, NY 12210
Tel: (518) 474-4429
http://www.dos.state.ny.us/lcns/professions/notary/notary1.htm

Binghamton
State Office Building
44 Hawley Street., Room 1506
Binghamton, NY 13901-4455
(607) 721-8757

Buffalo
65 Court Street, Room 208
Buffalo, NY 14202-3471
(716) 847-7110

Hauppauge
State Office Building
250 Veterans' Memorial Hwy.
Hauppauge, NY 11788-5519
(631) 952-6579

New York City
123 William Street, 19th Floor
New York, NY 10038-3804
(212) 417-5747

Syracuse
Hughes State Office Building
333 East Washington Street
Room 514
Syracuse, NY 13202-1428
(315) 428-4258

Utica
State Office Building
207 Genesee Street
Utica, NY 13501-2812
(315) 793-2533

County Clerks' Offices

Certified Copies. New York Notaries are not authorized by law to make certified copies. Persons requesting notarized or certified copies of marriage certificates or divorce decrees should be referred to the county clerk in the county where the marriage took place or the divorce was filed.

Oath and Application. Within two years of taking the Notary exam, the first-time Notary must file the exam slip, application and oath of office with the Department of State. Notaries seeking renewal should file the oath and application with their local county clerk's office.

Albany County
32 North Russell Road
Albany 12206-1324
(518) 487-5100

Allegany County
Courthouse
7 Court Street
Belmont, NY 14813
(585) 268-9270

Bronx County
851 Grand Concourse,
Bronx, NY 10451
(718) 590-3648

Broome County
44 Hawley Street
P.O. Box 2062
Binghamton, NY 13902
(607) 778-2272

Cattaraugus County
County Center
303 Court Street
Little Valley, NY 14755
(716) 938-9111

Cayuga County
County Office Bldg.
160 Genesee Street
Auburn, NY 13021
(315) 253-1271

Chautauqua County
County Court House
P.O. Box 170
Mayville, NY 14757
(716) 753-4331

Chemung County
210 Lake Street
P.O. Box 588
Elmira, NY 14902
(607) 737-2920

Chenango County
County Office Bldg.
5 Court Street
Norwich, NY 13815
(607) 337-1450

Clinton County
137 Margaret Street
Plattsburgh, NY 12901
(518) 565-4700

Columbia County
560 Warren Street
Hudson, NY 12534
(518) 828-3339

Cortland County
46 Greenbush Street
Suite 101
Cortland, NY
13045-3702
(607) 753-5021

Delaware County
P.O Box 426
Delhi, NY 13753
(607) 746-2123

Dutchess County
County Office Bldg.
22 Market Street
Poughkeepsie, NY
12601
(845) 486-2132

Erie County
25 Delaware Avenue
Buffalo, NY 14202
(716) 858-8865

Essex County
7559 Court Street
P.O. Box 247
Elizabethtown, NY
12932
(518) 873-3600

Franklin County
355 W. Main Street
P.O. Box 70
Malone, NY 12953
(518) 483-1681

Fulton County
P.O. Box 485
Johnstown, NY 12095
(518) 736-5555

Genesee County
15 Main Street
P.O. Box 379
Batavia, NY 14021
(585) 344-2550

Greene County
P.O. Box 446
Catskill, NY 12414
(518) 719-3255

Hamilton County
P.O. Box 204
Lake Pleasant, NY
12108
(518) 548-7111

Herkimer County
109 Mary Street
Suite 1111
Herkimer, NY 13350
(315) 867-1129

Jefferson County
County Bldg.
175 Arsenal Street
Watertown, NY 13601
(315) 785-3312

Kings County
360 Adams Street
Suite 188
Brooklyn, NY 11201
(718) 404-9750

Lewis County
P.O. Box 232
Lowville, NY 13367
(315) 376-5333

Livingston County
County Govt. Center
6 Court Street, Suite 201
Geneseo, NY 14454
(585) 243-7010

Madison County
County Office Bldg.
P.O. Box 668
Wampsville, NY 13163
(315) 366-2261

Monroe County
39 West Main Street
Rochester, NY 14614
(585) 753-1645

Montgomery County
County Office Bldg.
P.O. Box 1500
Fonda, NY 12068
(518) 853-8111

Nassau County
240 Old Country Road
Mineola, NY 11501
(516) 571-2661

New York City Register
66 John Street
13th Floor
New York, NY 10038
(212) 361-7130

New York County
60 Centre Street
Room 161
New York, NY 10007
(646) 386-5955

Niagara County
175 Hawley Street
P.O. Box 461
Lockport, NY 14094
(716) 439-7022

Oneida County
800 Park Avenue
Utica, NY 13501
(315) 798-5776

Onondaga County
Court House
401 Montgomery Street
Syracuse, NY 13202
(315) 435-2227

Ontario County
20 Ontario Street
Canandaigua, NY 14424
(585) 396-4200

Orange County
255 Main Street
Goshen, NY 10924
(845) 291-2690

Orleans County
Court House Square
3 South Main Street
Albion, NY 14411
(585) 589-5334

Oswego County
46 East Bridge Street
Oswego, NY 13126
(315) 349-8385

Otsego County
197 Main Street
P.O. Box 710
Cooperstown, NY
13326
(607) 547-4276

Putnam County
40 Gleneida Avenue
Carmel, NY 10512
(845) 225-3641

Queens County
88-11 Sutphin Blvd.
Jamaica, NY 11435
(718) 298-0601

Rensselaer County
105 Third Street
Troy, NY 12180
(518) 270-4080

Richmond County
130 Stuyvesant Place
Staten Island, NY
10301
(718) 390-5396

Rockland County
1 South Main Street,
Suite 100
New City, NY 10956
(845) 638-5221

St. Lawrence County
48 Court Street
Canton, NY 13617
(315) 379-2237

Saratoga County
40 McMaster Street
Ballston Spa, NY 12020
(518) 885-2213

Schenectady County
620 State Street
Schenectady, NY 12305
(518) 388-4222

Schoharie County
284 Main Street
P.O. Box 549
Schoharie, NY 12157
(518) 295-8316

Schuyler County
105 Ninth Street, Unit 8
Watkins Glen, NY
14891
(607) 535-8133

Seneca County
1 DiPronio Drive
Waterloo, NY 13165
(315) 539-1771

Steuben County
3 East Pulteney Square
Bath, NY 14810
(607) 776-9631

Suffolk County
310 Center Drive
Riverhead, NY 11901
(631) 852-2001

Sullivan County
Government Center
100 North Street
Monticello, NY 12701
(845) 794-3000

Tioga County
16 Court Street
P.O. Box 307.
Owego, NY 13827
(607) 687-8660

Tompkins County
320 North Tioga Street
Ithaca, NY 14850
(607) 274-5431

Ulster County
P.O. Box 1800
Kingston, NY 12402
(845) 340-3040

Warren County
1340 State Route 9
Lake George, NY
12845
(518) 761-6427

Washington County
Municipal Center
Upper Broadway
Fort Edward, NY 12828
(518) 746-2170

Wayne County
9 Pearl Street / P.O.
Box 608
Lyons, NY 14489
(315) 946-7470

Westchester County
110 Dr. Martin Luther
King Blvd.
White Plains, NY 10601
(914) 995-3081

Wyoming County
143 North Main Street,
Suite 104
Warsaw, NY 14569
(585) 786-8810

Yates County
417 Liberty Street
Suite 1107
Penn Yan, NY 14527
(315) 536-5120

Bureaus of Vital Statistics

Certified Copies. New York Notaries are not authorized by law to make certified copies. Persons requesting notarized or certified copies of birth or death certificates should be referred to the appropriate public Bureau of Vital Statistics. The following state agencies can provide certified copies of birth and death records for persons who were born or have died in the respective states or territories, as can certain local offices not listed here.

Alabama
Vital Records
Department of Public Health
P.O. Box 5625
Montgomery, AL 36103-5625

Alaska
Bureau of Vital Statistics
Department of Health &
Social Services
5441 Commercial Blvd.
P.O. Box 110675
Juneau, AK 99801

Arizona
Office of Vital Records
Department of Health Services
P.O. Box 3887
Phoenix, AZ 85030-3887

Arkansas
Division of Vital Records
Department of Health
4815 West Markham Street, Slot 44
Little Rock, AR 72205-3867

California
Office of Vital Records
Department of Health Services
P.O. Box 997410, MS: 5103
Sacramento, CA 95899-7410

Colorado
Vital Records Section
Department of Health
4300 Cherry Creek Drive South
Denver, CO 80246-1530

Connecticut
Department of Public Health
State Office of Vital Records
410 Capitol Avenue, MS #11VRS
P.O. Box 340308
Hartford, CT 06134-0308

Delaware
Health Statistics Center
Office of Vital Statistics
Jesse S. Cooper Building
417 Federal Street
Dover, DE 19901

District of Columbia
Vital Records Division
899 North Capitol Street NE,
1st Floor
Washington, DC 20002

Florida
Office of Vital Statistics
1217 North Pearl Street
P.O. Box 210
Jacksonville, FL 32231

Georgia
Vital Records
2600 Skyland Drive
Atlanta, GA 30319-3640

Hawaii
State Department of Health
Office of Health Status Monitoring
Issuance/Vital Statistics Section
P.O. Box 3378
Honolulu, HI 96801

Idaho
Vital Statistics Unit
450 West State Street, 1st Floor
P.O. Box 83720
Boise, ID 83720-0036

Illinois
Division of Vital Records
Department of Public Health
605 West Jefferson Street
Springfield, IL 62702-5097

Indiana
Vital Records Department
State Department of Health
2 North Meridian Street
Indianapolis, IN 46204

Iowa
Department of Public Health
Bureau of Vital Records
Lucas Office Building, 1st Floor
321 East 12th Street
Des Moines, IA 50319-0075

Kansas
Office of Vital Statistics
1000 SW Jackson Street, Suite 120
Topeka, KS 66612-2221

Kentucky
Office of Vital Statistics
Department for Health Services
275 East Main Street, 1E-A
Frankfort, KY 40621-0001

Louisiana
Vital Records Registry
P.O. Box 60630
New Orleans, LA 70160

Maine
Vital Statistics
220 Capitol Strect
11 State House Station
Augusta, ME 04333-0011

Maryland
Division of Vital Records
Department of Health
6550 Reisterstown Road
Baltimore, MD 21215

Massachusetts
Registry of Vital Records and
Statistics
150 Mount Vernon Street, 1st Floor
Dorchester, MA 02125-3105

Michigan
Vital Records Request
P.O. Box 30721
Lansing, MI 48909

Minnesota
Minnesota Department of Health
Central Cashiering — Vital Records
P.O. Box 64499
St. Paul, MN 55164-0499

Mississippi
Mississippi Vital Records
P.O. Box 1700
Jackson, MS 39215-1700

Missouri
Department of Health
Bureau of Vital Records
930 Wildwood
P.O. Box 570
Jefferson City, MO 65102-0570

Montana
Office of Vital Statistics
P.O. Box 4210
111 North Sanders, Room 6
Helena, MT 59604

Nebraska
Vital Statistics
Department of Health
1033 "O" Street, Suite 130
P.O. Box 95065
Lincoln, NE 68509-5065

Nevada
Office of Vital Records
4150 Technology Way, Suite 104
Carson City, NV 89706

New Hampshire
Department of State
Division of Vital Records
Administration
71 South Fruit Street
Concord, NH 03301-2410

New Jersey
Vital Statistics
Customer Service
P.O. Box 370
Trenton, NJ 08625-0370

New Mexico
Vital Records and Health Statistics
1105 South St. Francis Drive
Santa Fe, NM 87502

New York
State Department of Health
Vital Records Certification Unit
P.O. Box 2602
Albany, NY 12220-2602

New York City
NYC Department of Health and
Mental Hygiene
Office of Vital Records
125 Worth Street, CN4, Room 133
New York, NY 10013

North Carolina
Vital Records
1903 Mail Service Center
Raleigh, NC 27699-1903

North Dakota
Division of Vital Records
600 East Boulevard Avenue,
Dept. 301
Bismarck, ND 58505-0200

Ohio
Department of Health
Vital Statistics
P.O. Box 15098
Columbus, OH 43215-0098

Oklahoma
Vital Records Service
State Department of Health
1000 Northeast 10th Street
Oklahoma City, OK 73117

Oregon
Vital Records
P.O. Box 14050
Portland, OR 97293-0050

Pennsylvania
Division of Vital Records
101 South Mercer Street, Room 401
P.O. Box 1528
New Castle, PA 16101

Rhode Island
Office of Vital Records
Department of Health
3 Capitol Hill Road, Room 101
Providence, RI 02908-5097

South Carolina
Office of Vital Records
South Carolina DHEC
2600 Bull Street
Columbia, SC 29201

South Dakota
Vital Records
207 East Missouri Avenue, Suite 1A
Pierre, SD 57501

Tennessee
Tennessee Vital Records
1st Floor, Central Services Building
421 5th Avenue North
Nashville, TN 37243

Texas
Texas Vital Records
Department of State Health Services
P.O. Box 12040
Austin, TX 78711-2040

Utah
Vital Records and Statistics
Cannon Health Building
288 North 1460 West
P.O. Box 141012
Salt Lake City, UT 84114-1012

Vermont
Department of Health
Vital Records Section
108 Cherry Street
P.O. Box 70
Burlington, VT 05402-0070

Virginia
Office of Vital Records
P.O. Box 1000
Richmond, VA 23218-1000

Washington
Department of Health
Center for Health Statistics
P.O. Box 9709
Olympia, WA 98507-9709

West Virginia
Vital Registration
350 Capitol Street, Room 165
Charleston, WV 25301-3701

Wisconsin
Vital Records
1 West Wilson Street
P.O. Box 309
Madison, WI 53701-0309

Wyoming
Vital Statistics Services
Hathaway Building
Cheyenne, WY 82002

American Samoa
Office of Records and Vital Statistics
LBJ Tropical Medical Center
Department of Health Services
American Samoa Government
Pago Pago, AS 96799

Guam
Office of Vital Statistics
Department of Public Health
123 Chalan Kareta
Mangilao, GU, 96913

Northern Mariana Islands
Bureau of Health Planning
Statistics Office
P.O. Box 500409 CK
Saipan, MP 96950-0409

Panama Canal Zone
Passport Vital Records Office
U.S. Department of State
1111 19th Street NW, Suite 510
Washington, DC 20036

Puerto Rico
Department of Health
Demographic Registry
P.O. Box 11854
Fernández Juncos Station
San Juan, PR 00910

Virgin Islands (St. Croix)
Department of Health
Vital Statistics
Charles Harwood Memorial Hospital
St. Croix, VI 00820

**Virgin Islands
(St. Thomas, St. John)**
Department of Health
Registrar of Vital Statistics
Knud Hansen Complex
St. Thomas, VI 0080

Hague Convention Nations

The nations listed on the following pages are parties to a treaty called *The Hague Convention Abolishing the Requirement of Legalization for Foreign Public Documents*, hereafter simply called the Hague Convention.

Treaty Simplifies Authentication. A Notary's signature on documents that are sent to these nations may be authenticated (verified as valid for the benefit of the recipient in the foreign nation) through attachment of an authentication certificate called an *apostille* (French for "notation"). Nations not subscribing to the Hague Convention may require as many as five or six separate authentication certificates from different governmental agencies, domestic and foreign.

Usually, the *apostille* is the only authentication certificate necessary for documents destined for a Hague-Convention nation. The New York Department of State, however, requires the notarized document to bear an authentication certificate from the county clerk in the county in which the document was notarized before it will issue an *apostille*.

How to Request an *Apostille*. To obtain an *apostille*, anyone may mail or present the notarized document, the county clerk's authentication certificate and a $10 check, payable to "New York Department of State," to:

Department of State
State Records Bureau
One Commerce Plaza
99 Washington Avenue
Albany, NY 12231-0001
(518) 473-1001

Department of State
Certification Unit
123 William Street, 19th Floor
New York, NY 10038-3804
(212) 417-5747

An *apostille* must be specifically requested, and the nation to which the document will be sent must be indicated. It is not the Notary's responsibility to obtain an *apostille*; it is the responsibility of the party requesting authentication.

Hague Convention Nations. The nations listed below participate in the Hague Convention. Footnotes reflect information most likely to be of interest to Notaries acting in the United States and its territories. Please note that some nations listed may not recognize the participation of every other nation listed. To verify recognition between nations, consult the website of the Hague Conference on Private International Law at http://www.hcch.net/index_en.php.

Albania	Botswana[13]	Fiji[13]
Andorra[13]	Brunei Darussalam[13]	Finland
Antigua and	Bulgaria	France[4]
Barbuda[13]	Cape Verde[13]	Georgia[5]
Argentina[1]	Colombia[13]	Germany[8]
Armenia[13]	Cook Islands[13]	Greece
Australia	Costa Rica	Grenada[13]
Austria	Croatia[2]	Honduras[13]
Azerbaijan[13]	Cyprus	Hong Kong[6]
Bahamas[13]	Czech Republic	Hungary
Bahrain[13]	Denmark[3]	Iceland
Barbados[13]	Dominica[13]	India
Belarus	Dominican	Ireland
Belgium[8]	Republic[13]	Israel
Belize[13]	Ecuador	Italy
Bosnia and	El Salvador[13]	Japan
Herzegovina[2]	Estonia	Kazakhstan[13]

1. Argentina does not recognize the extension of the Convention by the United Kingdom to the Malvinas (Falkland Islands), South Georgia, South Sandwich Islands and the Argentine Antarctic Sector (British Antarctic Territory). See n. 11.
2. The former Socialist Federal Republic of Yugoslavia was a party to the Convention. Only the successor states of Bosnia and Herzegovina, Croatia, the Republic of Macedonia, Montenegro, Serbia and Slovenia have confirmed that the Convention still applies.
3. The participation of Denmark does not extend to Greenland and the Faro Islands.
4. The participation of France is extended to the entire territory of the French Republic, including French Guyana, French Polynesia, Guadeloupe, Martinique, Mayotte, New Caledonia, Reunion, St. Barthelemy, St. Martin, St. Pierre and Miquelon, and Wallis and Futuna.
5. The participation of Georgia does not extend to Abkhazia and South Ossetia.
6. Hong Kong and Macao retained their status as Hague nations after control was returned to China on July 1, 1997 (Hong Kong) and December 20, 1999 (Macao).
7. The participation of New Zealand does not extend to Tokelau.
8. The Convention does not apply between Liberia and the United States, Belgium or Germany.
9. The participation of the Netherlands is extended to Aruba and the Netherlands Antilles.
10. The participation of Portugal is extended to the entire territory of the Republic of Portugal, including the Azores and Madeira.

Korea, Republic of	Netherlands[9]	Serbia[2]
Kyrgyzstan[13,14]	New Zealand[7]	Seychelles[13]
Latvia	Nicaragua	Slovakia
Lesotho[13]	Niue[13]	Slovenia[2]
Liberia[8,13]	Norway	South Africa
Liechtenstein[13]	Oman[13]	Spain[17]
Lithuania	Panama	Suriname
Luxembourg	Peru[16]	Swaziland[13]
Macao[6]	Poland	Sweden
Macedonia[2]	Portugal[10]	Switzerland
Malawi[13]	Romania	Tonga[13]
Malta	Russian Federation	Trinidad and
Marshall Islands[13]	Saint Kitts and	Tobago[13]
Mauritius[13]	Nevis[13]	Turkey
Mexico	Saint Lucia[13]	Ukraine
Moldova, Republic	Saint Vincent and	United Kingdom[1,11]
of[13,18]	the Grenadines[13]	United States[8,12]
Monaco	Samoa[13]	Uruguay
Mongolia[13,19]	San Marino[13]	Uzbekistan[13,15]
Montenegro[2]	Sao Tome and	Vanuatu[13]
Namibia[13]	Principe[13]	Venezuela

Inquiries. Persons having questions about *The Hague Convention Abolishing the Requirement of Legalization for Foreign Public Documents* may address their inquiries to:

U.S. Department of State
Authentication Office
518 23rd Street, NW
State Annex 1
Washington, DC 20520
(202) 647-5002

---

11. The participation of the United Kingdom of Great Britain and Northern Ireland is extended to Anguilla, Bermuda, British Antarctic Territory, British Virgin Islands, Cayman Islands, Falkland Islands, Gibraltar, Guernsey, Isle of Man, Jersey, Montserrat, St. Helena and Turks and Caicos Islands.
12. The United States includes American Samoa, District of Columbia, Guam, Northern Mariana Islands, Puerto Rico and U.S. Virgin Islands.
13. This nation is not a member of the Hague Conference on Private International Law but is a party to *The Hague Convention Abolishing the Requirement of Legalization for Foreign Public Documents*.
14. The Convention will not enter into force between Kyrgyzstan and Austria, Belgium, Germany, or Greece.
15. The Convention will not enter into force between Uzbekistan and Austria, Belgium, Germany, or Greece.
16. The Convention will not enter into force between Peru and Germany or Greece.
17. The Ministry of Justice of Spain has put in place a new system for the issuance of *Apostilles*, which includes the possibility to issue both electronic and paper *Apostilles* (Note dated 23 June 2011).
18. The Convention will not enter into force between Moldova and Germany.
19. The Convention will not enter into force between Mongolia and Austria, Belgium, Finland, Germany, or Greece.

About the NNA

Since 1957, the National Notary Association — a nonprofit educational organization — has served the nation's Notaries Public with a wide variety of instructional programs and services.

As the country's clearinghouse for information on Notary laws, customs and practices, the NNA educates Notaries through publications, seminars, webinars, online training, annual conferences, its website and the NNA Hotline that offers immediate answers to specific questions about notarization.

The Association is perhaps most widely known as the preeminent source of information for and about Notaries. NNA works include the following:

- *The National Notary*, a magazine for NNA members featuring how-to articles and practical tips on notarizing

- *Notary Bulletin*, an online newsletter that keeps NNA members and customers up to date on developments affecting Notaries, especially new state laws and regulations

- *Sorry, No Can Do!* series, four volumes that help Notaries explain to customers and bosses why some requests for notarizations are improper and cannot be accommodated

- *U.S. Notary Reference Manual*, an invaluable resource for any person relying upon the authenticity and correctness of legal documents

- *Notary Public Practices & Glossary*, a definitive reference book on notarial procedures and widely hailed as the Notary's bible

- State *Notary Law Primers*, short guidebooks that explain a state's Notary statutes in easy-to-understand language

- *The Notary Public Code of Professional Responsibility*, a comprehensive and detailed code of ethical and professional conduct for Notaries

- *The Model Notary Act*, prototype legislation conceived in 1973 and updated in 1984, 2002 and 2010 by an NNA-recruited panel of secretaries of state, legislators and attorneys, and regularly used by state legislatures in revising their Notary laws

- *Notary Signing Agent Training Course*, a manual covering every aspect of signing agent procedures that prepares candidates for the Notary Signing Agent Certification Examination developed by the NNA

- Public-service pamphlets informing the general public about the function of a Notary, including *What Is A Notary Public?* printed in English and Spanish

In addition, the NNA offers the highest quality professional supplies, including official seals and stamps, embossers, recordkeeping journals, jurat stamps, thumbprinting devices and notarial certificates.

Though dedicated primarily to educating and assisting Notaries, the NNA supports implementing effective Notary laws and informing the public about the Notary's vital role in modern society. ■

Index

Page numbers listed in **bold** indicate where the most complete information on a subject can be found. *Italics* indicate the pages where the statutes pertaining to a subject are located.

Page numbers listed in **bold** indicate where the most complete information on a subject can be found. *Italics* indicate the pages where the statutes pertaining to a subject are located.

NOTES